SERMONS ON
BIBLICAL CHARACTERS

SERMONS ON
BIBLICAL CHARACTERS

CLOVIS G. CHAPPELL

BAKER BOOK HOUSE
Grand Rapids, Michigan 49506

50 56

Originally published in 1922 by
George H. Doran Company

Reprinted 1970, 1981 by
Baker Book House Company

ISBN: 0-8010-2330-0

Printed in the United States of America

CONTENTS

SERMONS ON
BIBLICAL CHARACTERS

I

THE MISSING MAN—THOMAS

John 20:24

"Thomas, one of the twelve, called Didymus, was not with them when Jesus came." Did you notice the name of this man who was missing? Who was it when the little company met after the crucifixion that was not there? There was a man expected who failed to come. Who was this man? When the little company gathered in the upper room behind shut doors there was one chair that was vacant. Who should have occupied that chair?

Well, in the first place, it was not Judas. He was missing. He was not there, it is true, but he was not expected. Judas had already betrayed his Lord. Judas had already been whipped and scourged by his remorse of conscience clean out of the world. Judas had gone to his own place in the great Unseen Country. Judas was not there, but he was not expected to be there.

Who was the missing man? It was not Pilate. We no more expected Pilate than we expected Judas. Pilate had had his chance at Jesus. Pilate had had an opportunity of knowing, of befriending Him, of serving Him. But Pilate had allowed his own interests to get the better of his conscience. Pilate had chosen the friendship of Cæsar and had spurned the friend- ship of the King Eternal. So we did not expect Pilate to be present in this little company of the friends of Jesus who met on the resurrection side of the cross. Who was the missing man? It was not Caiaphas. He, too, had stood in the presence of Jesus, but his envy had made him blind. And he shouted "Blasphemy!" so loud that he drowned the voice of his conscience and the gentle whisperings of the Spirit of God. No, it was not Caiaphas, nor any of the indifferent or hostile crowd that we miss in this meeting.

Then, who was this missing man? And we read the text again and we find his name was Thomas. That is a very familiar name. Oh, yes; we remember Thomas quite well. It was Thomas who was missing. Now, Thomas was expected, for he was a member of the little band of disciples. He was one of the Twelve. He belonged to the Inner Circle. His fellow Christians had a right therefore to expect him. Yet Thomas was not with them.

It is a sad day ever for any congregation when its own membership begin to absent themselves from its services. It is a sad day for any congregation when those who compose it can be counted on to be there at the social function, there at the place of business, but cannot be counted on when the interests of the Kingdom are at stake and when the Son of God goes forth to war. Believe me, no community ever loses respect for a congregation till that congregation loses respect for itself.

And did you notice when it was that Thomas was absent? "Thomas was not with them when Jesus came." What an unfortunate time to be away! What a great calamity to have missed that service of all others! There was the little despondent, despairing company of ten meeting behind closed doors. They were sorrow-burdened and fear-filled. But Jesus came, and Thomas, the saddest and bitterest man of them all, was not there.

Of course he would have gone if he had had any idea what a wonderful service it was going to be. If he had even dreamed that Jesus would be there, of course he would not have missed it; but he expected the meeting to be a very dull affair. He felt confident that whoever else was there that there would be no Christ. He expected that Peter and James and John and the rest would meet there and talk of a glorious past that had gone forever. He would have said, "Yes, I know what they will say. They will tell how Jesus called them at the beginning. They will tell how they forsook all to follow Him. They will tell of the great dreams that they dreamed, of the high hopes that they cherished. They will tell of all the glad, radiant days that have 'dropped into the sunset.' But they will have nothing to say to relieve the bitterness of to-day or to fling a bow of hope upon the black skies of to-morrow. So I will not go to the meeting to-day."

But the meeting was not dull. The meeting was not sad. The meeting was not a lament for a glory that was passed, for a glad day that had slipped behind them forever more. It was a service that thrilled with present joys. It was a meeting that made the future to glow with glorious possibilities. It was wonderful, because Jesus came. He came then, and He comes still. Wherever hungry hearts come together who yearn for Him and make Him welcome, there comes the blessed Christ to stand in the midst. And therefore I would not absent myself from the meeting together of the people of God. I would not because I want to be there when Jesus comes, when the King comes in to see the guests.

"Thomas was not with them when Jesus came." I wonder why it was that Thomas was missing. I wonder how it came about that he, the neediest man among the apostles, was not there to receive the inspiration and the uplift that came from this service. Why was he not there?

It was not, I am sure, because he was indifferent. There are many to-day who have separated themselves from the services of the church, from the fellowship of the saints, because of a deadening indifference. They have become absorbed in a thousand other matters till they have become doubly uninterested in the things of the church and in the affairs of the Kingdom.

Thomas was not missing because he had found satisfaction elsewhere. Thomas was not satisfied. Thomas was not happy. I doubt if there was a sadder man in all Jerusalem than Thomas. I doubt if there was a more wretched man in the wide world at that time than was Thomas. Thomas had not turned aside from Jesus to satisfy his soul on husks. He had not left Christ because his needs had been met and his thirst satisfied at some other fountain.

Why was Thomas missing? He was missing because he had lost hope. He believed that Christ was dead. He believed that the cause for which he had stood was lost and lost forever more. He believed that right was forever defeated; that wrong was forever enthroned. Over his head was a blackened sky. For him there was not one single ray of light nor one single gleam of hope.

If I had met Thomas on the streets of Jerusalem on that day and said, "Thomas, I saw your friends going together to the Upper Room. Aren't you going? Jesus might come while they are there," Thomas would have answered, "No, I'm not going. Jesus will not be there. He is dead. Don't you know if I thought I would see Him I would go? Don't you know that I loved Him and love Him still better than life, but Jesus is dead. Dead! Dead!

"I was in the garden when Judas kissed Him. I saw them lead Him away. I saw the soldiers scourge Him. I saw Him crowned with the crown of thorns. I was out on Calvary when the black night came on at midday and I heard that wild, bitter cry. Oh! I will hear it forever more: 'My God, my God, why hast thou forsaken me?' I saw His head bowed and I saw the brute of a soldier thrust the spear into His side. Don't talk to me about seeing Jesus again. Jesus is dead."

The very bitterness of the sorrow of Thomas had driven him to despair. He found it hard to believe always. Here he found it impossible. Now, there are some folks who are sweetened by sorrow and made better. There are others that are made bitter and morose and despairful. I heard a man cry one day, an awful cry: "Oh, I could curse God," he said, "if I knew there was a God, for letting little Mary die!" For Thomas everything had collapsed. There was not a star in his sky. There was not a horizon in his life in which he might hope for a dawn. So that he, the neediest man of them all, was not there when Jesus came.

And now, will you see what he missed. Truly, the man was right who did not wonder what people suffered, but wondered at what they missed. And just see what this man Thomas missed by not being in the little meeting among the ten. First, he missed the privilege of seeing Jesus. He missed the privilege of seeing Him who had throttled Death and hell and the grave and had brought life and immortality to light through the Gospel. He missed seeing Him, one vision of whose face would have changed his sobbing into singing and his night into marvelous day.

He missed seeing Jesus, and failing to see Him, he missed the glorious certainty of the after life. It is Christ, my friends, that makes Heaven and the eternal life sure for us. It is He who enables men to go down into the great silence without a doubt and without a fear. It is He who makes us absolutely confident that there is a Home of the Soul, that—

> "There is a land of pure delight
> Where saints immortal reign."

Having seen Him once dead and alive forever more, we have no slightest doubt of the truth of His promise that, because He lives we shall live also.

By staying away that day Thomas missed the thrill of a great joy. Had he been there he might have seen the Lord. This is not a possibility in every service, possibly, but it ought to be. It is a possibility in every successful service. I heard of a preacher once who thought that what his congregation wanted was beautiful epigrams. He thought that they were more hungry for bejeweled verbiage than for the Bread of Life. He thought they were thirsting more for a stream of eloquence than for the Water of Life. But he was mistaken. And once he came into the pulpit to find a card lying before him on which was written this word: "Sir, we would know Jesus."

At first it angered him a bit and then it made him think. And then it sent him to his knees. And then it sent him into the pulpit with a new message. And one day he came again into his pulpit to find a second card before him. Picking it up, he read these words: "Then were the disciples glad when they saw the Lord." Of course they were. Their gladness was the gladness of the ten that met in the Upper Room. Their gladness was the gladness that might have been experienced by Thomas. It was intended for him, for he was the saddest and most wretched man in Jerusalem. But Thomas was not there.

Thomas missed also the gift of peace. Jesus said to those present, "Peace be unto you." And how Thomas needed that gift! Thomas was in a fever of restlessness and wretchedness. He was whipped by a veritable tempest of doubt and utter unbelief. And all the while he might have had the peace that passeth understanding. He might have had the vision of Him who stood then, and still stands, the central figure of the ages, saying, "Come unto me, all ye that labor and are heavy laden, and I will give you rest." Those present that day were blessed with the gift of peace. They had "fervor without fever." They had motion without friction. But Thomas missed it because "he was not with them when Jesus came."

The disciples who were there were re-commissioned that day. Jesus said to them, "As the Father hath sent me, even so send I you." With His death everything seemed at an end. The great program that He had given them seemed to have lapsed forever. A man said a few years ago, "Life doesn't seem worth living since I found that Christianity is not true." It was so with these men. They were men without a goal. But Jesus came and recommissioned them, laid upon them again the high task of conquering the world. And Thomas missed that great blessing because he was not there.

Last of all, Jesus breathed upon them and said, "Receive ye the Holy Ghost." These men were not only recommissioned. They received the Holy Ghost. "He breathed on them." How close they came to Him that day! How their hearts were warmed! How their hopes were revived! "He breathed on them and said, Receive ye the Holy Ghost." And poor Thomas missed also this benediction because he was not with them when Jesus came.

It may be that you were once active in the church. It may be that you were once a live and enthusiastic Christian. But little by little you have slipped back. You have moved to strange places. Your life has been thrown in great cities. And you have missed the fellowships of yesterday out of your life. It may be that to-day you are no longer found regularly among the worshipers in God's House. You are missing something. Don't deceive yourself. As the saints of God meet together Jesus still manifests Himself. And seeing Him, there comes to us a new joy and peace, a new sense of the purpose and worthfulness of life. Seeing Him there comes to us a new power for battle and for conquest.

But if we have missed Him, whatever else we have won, we have missed about all that is worth while. Oh, there is one thing of which I am absolutely sure, and that is that if I have Jesus, if His presence is a gladsome reality to my heart, nothing else matters much. But if I miss Him everything goes wrong and everything is disappointing. Darius is in the palace and Daniel in the den of lions, but there is restlessness and wretchedness in the palace and peace and joy in the lions' den. It is the presence of God that makes the difference.

Thomas, because he missed receiving, also missed the privilege of giving. When the other disciples came from that meeting, how radiant were their faces! What a spring they had in their step! What joy bringers they were! What a marvelously thrilling story they had to tell! Freely had they received and freely did they give.

But Thomas. He had received nothing, therefore he had nothing to give. He was a disappointment to his Master. For a whole week he went doubting Him, mistrusting Him, when it was his privilege to have walked into His fellowship and been as sure of His reality and of His nearness as he was of his own existence.

In the second place, he missed the privilege of helping his fellow disciples. What an encouragement he might have been to them! How it would have strengthened the faith of those Christians who had not yet seen the vision of their risen Lord to have seen the light even upon the gloomy face of Thomas! But Thomas missed the privilege of giving. I cannot rob myself without robbing you. I cannot starve myself spiritually without helping to starve you. I cannot sin alone. If I do that which lowers my spiritual vitality, by that very act I help to lower yours also. "Thomas was not with them when Jesus came," and he missed a double blessing, the privilege of receiving and the privilege of giving.

But Thomas, in spite of his failure, succeeded in the end. Tradition tells us that he died a martyr for his love and devotion to his Lord. How was he saved? How was he brought to the joy and usefulness that are born of certainty? Thomas, you know, was a doubter. A very thoroughgoing doubter he was. How then, in spite of his doubts, did he find his way into the fulness of the Light?

First, Thomas was not proud of his doubts. He did not look upon them as blessings or as treasures. There is a type of doubter to-day who does. I have heard men speak of "my doubts" as if they were very priceless things. But no man is of necessity the richer for his doubts. I know that doubt may become a doorway to a larger faith. Still, I repeat, no man is of necessity the richer for them. For instance, no man is the richer because of his social doubts. The man who does not believe in his fellow man is poor indeed. The man who has doubts about the inmates of his home suffers something of the pangs of hell. And the man who doubts God can hardly consider himself the possessor of a prize to be coveted. Thomas doubted, but he was not proud of his doubts.

Thomas was not only not proud of his doubts, but was thoroughly wretched on account of them. And being thoroughly wretched because of them, he was willing to be set right. He wanted to believe. It seems to me that any man would. Thomas was eager to be made sure that the Christ he loved was really alive. He yearned for certainty.

Thomas was not only willing, but Thomas was reasonable. When he sought to be sure of Jesus he put himself in the best possible position to learn the truth. When he wanted to be made sure of Christ he did

not seek knowledge at the hands of the enemies of
Christ. He did not ask information of those who
were confessed strangers to Christ. So often we do.
We get in the grip of doubt and straightway we turn
from the fellowship of those who know the Lord to
the fellowship of those who confessedly do not know
Him. We read those books that strengthen our doubts
rather than those that strengthen our faith. But
Thomas was wiser.

"Thomas, we have seen the Lord." That is what
Peter and James and John and the rest said to Thomas
after this wonderful service that Thomas missed. And
what was the answer of this doubter? Did his face
light up as he said, "I am glad to hear it"? Not a
bit of it. He said, "Except I see in His hand the
print of the nails and put my finger into the print of
the nails and thrust my hand into His side I will not
believe." And what Thomas meant by this answer
was simply this: "There is nothing that you can say
or do that will make me believe at all. I simply cannot
believe and cannot be made to believe that Jesus has
risen."

Now I do not think that his fellow disciples argued
with him. Really it would have done no good. They
simply left him to his own thoughts. And I fancy
that those thoughts ran something after this fashion:
"What they say is not true. They are mistaken. Of
course they are. They must be. And yet they certainly believe in the truth of what they say. God
grant that they are right. There is nothing that I
would not give to know."

Then what did this honest and earnest doubter do?
Listen! "And after eight days again the disciples
were within and Thomas with them." Yes, Thomas is

a doubter. But he is an honest and hungry-hearted doubter. He is willing to give himself every opportunity to know the truth. He says, "I will turn my face toward the east. Then if there is a dawn I will see it." And what happened? The dawning came. The sun rose, "even the Son of righteousness with healing in His wings." "Then came Jesus, the doors being shut, and stood in the midst, and said, Peace be unto you. Then saith He to Thomas, Reach hither thy finger and behold my hands, and reach hither thy hand, and thrust it into my side; and be not faithless, but believing. And Thomas answered and said unto Him, My Lord and my God."

Thomas became absolutely certain. It is my firm conviction that that same certainty is your privilege and mine. I believe that Jesus spoke the simple truth when He said, "If any man is willing to do His will, he shall know." However little you may believe at this present moment, if you will be loyal to what you do believe, if you will follow the light that you have, it will bring you into the brightness of the day.

You remember how Horace Bushnell, while a student at Yale, felt that he was in the way of a great revival that was sweeping through the University. He did not want to stand in the way of this revival and yet he was an unbeliever. He did not feel that he could come out on the side of Jesus Christ for he did not believe in Christ. "What then do you believe?" a voice within him seemed to ask. "I believe there is an absolute difference between right and wrong," was the answer. "Have you ever put yourself on the side of the right to follow it regardless of consequences?" was the next question. "I have not," was the answer, "but I will." So Horace Bushnell kneeled there in his room and dedicated himself to the service of the right. And what was the result? After he had been a preacher of the Gospel in Hartford, Connecticut, for forty-seven years he said, "Better than I know any man in Hartford I know Jesus Christ."

When I was a lad I was overtaken by darkness while some eight or ten miles from home. The night was intensely black, so much so that I lost my way absolutely. I found myself after some hours in a dense forest. I made up my mind to dismount from my horse and sleep on the ground, as I saw no chance of finding my way home.

But I had no sooner dismounted than the lightning began to flash and the thunder to roar and I was warned of an approaching storm. A little later the storm burst upon me. And I mounted and rode on through the dark, not knowing whither I went. At last, far past midnight, I saw a speck of light in the distance. That light did not look at all like a sunrise. It was as small as a needle point. And yet I followed it because it was all I could see on the black bosom of the darkness. A little later I found that that light was shining from a window in my own home. A little later still I found my anxious mother behind that light waiting for the home-coming of her boy.

Now, I did not have much light to begin with. It was pathetically meager. But as I followed it it led me home. Thomas had but little. Bushnell had but little. But they were willing to be true to the light that they had. And being true to it, they found the fullness of the light. For it was true then as it is true to-day, "if any man is willing to do His will, he shall know."

II

THE GREAT REFUSAL—JONAH

Jonah 1:1-3

There is doubtless not another book in the literature of the world that has suffered more at the hands of men than the book of Jonah. It has been tortured by its enemies and wounded in the house of its friends. We have been so prone to give our attention to the non-essential in the book rather than the essential. We have had such keen eyes for the seemingly ridiculous and the bizarre. For this reason it has come to pass that you can hardly mention the name of Jonah to a modern audience without provoking a smile. Thus Jonah, coming to us as an evangelist, is mistaken by many for a clown.

Now this is a calamity. It is a calamity in the first place because the book of Jonah is one of the gems of literature. There is not another book in the Old Testament that is more fragrant with the breath of inspiration. There is not another book more radiant with the light of the divine love. It is a wonderful gospel in itself. Therefore it is a great pity that we have turned from its winsome wealth to give ourselves to the unedifying task of measuring the size of a fish's throat.

Did you ever hear of the hungry men that were invited to a feast? When they came within the banquet hall they found the table spread with the viands of a king. But the table was a bit out of the ordinary.

22

Therefore, there arose a discussion over the material out of which it was made. These guests began heated arguments also over the method of its carpentry. And they argued so long and learnedly and well that the food went utterly to waste and they went away more hungry than when they had come.

There is a story of a prince who loved a beautiful peasant girl. In spite of his royal blood he determined to marry her. To seal his pledge of marriage he sent her a wonderful engagement ring. It was a gem so marvelous that it was said the stars shut their eyes in its presence and even the sun acknowledged it as a rival. But the girl was more interested in the beautiful box in which it was packed than she was in the ring. And when the prince came he was humiliated and disappointed to find her wearing the box tied upon her finger while the jewel had been neglected and forgotten and utterly lost.

Now there is real jewelry here. Let us forget the rather queer casket in which this jewel comes while we examine the treasure. "The word of the Lord came unto Jonah the son of Ammittai, saying, Arise, go to Nineveh, that great city, and cry against it; for its wickedness has come up before me." "The word of the Lord came unto Jonah." There is nothing crude about that statement. There is nothing in that to excite our ridicule. That is one of the blessed and thrilling truths of the ages. To this man Jonah, living some time, somewhere, God spoke. To this man God made known His will and holy purpose.

And God is speaking still. The word of God is coming to men and women to-day. There is not a single soul listening to me at this moment but what at some time in your life there has come a definite and sure

word from God. You have felt the impress of His
Spirit upon your own spirit. You have felt the touch
of His hand on yours. You have seen His finger
pointing to the road in which you ought to walk and
to the task that He was calling upon you to perform.

How this word came to Jonah we do not know, nor
do we need to know. It may have come to him
through the consciousness of another's need. It may
have come to him through a study of the Word. It
may have come to him through the call of a friend.
How it came is not the essential thing. The one thing
essential and fundamental is this, that the word did
come. That is the essential thing in your case and
in mine. God does speak to us. God does move upon
us. God does call us, command us. God does stir
us up. "The word of the Lord came unto Jonah," and
it comes this very moment to you and to me.

What was it that the Lord said to Jonah? He gave
him a strange and unwelcome command. He said,
"Arise and go to Nineveh, that great city, and cry
against it, for its wickedness has come up before me."
It was hard for Jonah to believe that he had heard
aright. Was it possible that Nineveh was a great
city in spite of the fact that it was a heathen city?
Was it possible that Nineveh grieved God because of
its wickedness? Could it be possible that God really
loved Nineveh, though it was outside the covenant?
Jonah did not want to believe this, but he had to
believe it. He had to realize that

"The love of God is wider than the measure of man's mind
    And the heart of the Eternal is most wonderfully kind."

Jonah did not want to undertake this mission. His
objection, however, did not grow out of the fear that

Nineveh would refuse to repent. His reluctance was not born of the conviction that there was nothing in the people of Nineveh to which his message would appeal. I know we are often hampered by that conviction. We feel that it is absolutely useless to preach to some folks. There is no use in trying to christianize Africa. There is no use even in trying to christianize some of our next door neighbors. We so often forget that there is in every man an insatiable hunger and an unquenchable thirst that none but God can satisfy.

But to Jonah this call was unwelcome because he feared that Nineveh might repent. And that he did not want Nineveh to do. Jonah believed that God was the God of Israel only. He believed that God blessed Israel in two ways. First, He blessed her by giving her gifts spiritual and temporal. And He blessed her, in the second place, by sending calamities upon her enemies. An abundant harvest in Israel was a blessing from the Lord. A famine in Nineveh was also a blessing from the Lord. Jonah was firmly convinced that the prosperity of a nation other than his own meant calamity to Israel.

It is a pity that this selfish belief did not perish with Jonah. But when we face the facts we know that it did not. It is a very human trait in us to feel that another's advancement is in some way a blow to ourselves. It is equally a human trait to feel that another's downfall and disgrace in some way adds a bit of luster to our own crowns. Of course, nothing could be more utterly false, but in spite of this fact we cling to that faith through all the passing centuries.

On the whole this duty, then, that God had put upon Jonah was so distasteful that he made up his mind that whatever it might cost him he would not obey.

Therefore, we read that he "rose up to flee unto Tarshish from the presence of the Lord." Ordered to Nineveh he sets out for Tarshish. There were two cities on his map and only two. There was Nineveh, the city to which he might go in the fellowship of God and within the circle of the will of God. There was also Tarshish, the city that lay at the end of the rebel's road, the city whose streets, if ever he walked them at all, he would walk without the fellowship of the God whom he had disobeyed.

And there are just two cities on your map. The Nineveh of obedience and the Tarshish of disobedience. You are going to Nineveh or to Tarshish. I do not claim to know where your Nineveh is. It may be a distant city. It may be a city across the seas whose streets you will crimson with the blood of your sacrifice. It may be a city as near to you as the home in which you live, as the child that nestles in your arms. But wherever it is, if you walk its streets you will walk them in the joy of the divine fellowship.

On the other hand, you may go to Tarshish. Tarshish is the city of "Have-Your-Own-Way." It is the city of "Do-As-You-Please." It is the city of "Take-it-Easy." It is the city with no garden called Gethsemane without its gates and no rugged hill called Calvary overlooks its walls. It is a city without a cross and yet it is a city where people seldom sing and often sob. It is a city where nobody looks joyously into God's face and calls Him Father.

I met Jonah that day on the wharf. He looked like he had passed through a terrible spell of sickness. His cheeks were hollow. His eyes were red with sleeplessness. He had a haggard, worn, hounded look about him. "Are you on the way home, Jonah?" And he shook

his head and said, "No. I am going to Tarshish."
Tarshish was the most far away place of which the Jew
had any conception. "Tarshish!" I say in astonishment. "What are you going to do over at Tarshish?"
"Oh," he said, "I hadn't thought about that. I do not
know what the future has in store for me. What I am
trying to do is to get away from God." "And Jonah
arose to flee unto Tarshish from the presence of the
Lord."

I wonder why the text did not say "And Jonah
arose to flee unto Tarshish from the presence of his
duty" instead of "from the presence of the Lord."
The writer of this story had real spiritual insight.
He was far clearer in his thinking than many of us.
He knew that to flee from duty was to flee from God.
Whenever you make up your mind to refuse to go
where God wants you to go and to do what God wants
you to do, you must make up your mind at the same
time to renounce the friendship of God. You cannot
walk with Him and at the same time be in rebellion
against Him. God has no possible way of entering into
fellowship with the soul that is disobedient to His will.
Believe me, it is absolutely useless, it is mere mockery,
to say "Lord, Lord" and then refuse to do the things
that He commands you to do.

Now, when Jonah saw the spaces of water growing
wider between him and the shore a kind of deadly calm
came upon him. A man with his mind made up to
do wrong is far more at rest than the man whose mind
is not made up at all. So when Jonah had fully decided that he would rebel against God and give up all
claim to God, a dreadful restfulness came to his troubled spirit. He went down into the sides of the ship
and went fast asleep. The days before had been trou-

bled days. The nights had been restless nights. But the battle was over now, even though it had been lost, and he was able at last to sleep.

This period marks, I am sure, the period of greatest danger in the life of Jonah. Jonah had been a rebel before, but he had been a restless rebel. He had been disobedient before, but his disobedience had tortured him. It had put strands of gray into his hair and wrinkles upon his brow. But now he is not only in rebellion, but he is content to be so. He is not only without God, but he is, in a measure, satisfied to be without Him. No greater danger can come to any man than that. As long as your sin breaks your heart, as long as your disobedience makes you lie awake nights and wet your pillow in tears there is hope for you. But when you become contented with your wickedness, when you come to believe that it is the best possible for you, then you are in danger indeed.

Now, I am fully convinced that Jonah's danger is the danger of a great many, both in the Church and out. You who are listening to me at this moment are kindly and cultured men and women. You are full of good will toward the Church. You love it and desire its prosperity. Yet many of you are doing practically nothing to make its desired prosperity a reality. One of the most discouraging features about the Church to-day is the large number of utterly useless people within its fold. And these are not only useless, but saddest of all, they are content with their uselessness. They seem to feel that it is God's best for them; that it is all that God expects or has a right to expect.

Did you ever make out your religious program and look at it? What does discipleship cost you? What is involved in your allegiance to the Lord? Coming to

church once or twice a month on Sunday mornings
and making a small contribution. Only this and nothing more. The Sunday School is not your burden.
The prayer meeting is not your burden. Visiting the
new members that have recently come into our Church
and into the Kingdom and need your help is not your
responsibility. Helping by your presence and by your
prayers to give spiritual fervor to all the services, is
not your responsibility. Yours is to make your way
up to the doors of the House of Many Mansions by and
by without ever having made one single costly sacrifice
in order to follow the Lord.

Are you running away from your duty this morning? You know what it is. At least you may know
it. This is a needy world. This is a needy Church.
It has an opportunity to touch the uttermost parts of
the earth if it is spiritually alive and spiritually
mighty. Are you making your contribution? Are
you accepting your responsibility or have you turned
your back upon it for no other reason than just
this, that it is too much trouble? If that is true of
me and if that is true of you, may the Lord wake us
up this morning and give us to see our deadly danger.

So Jonah turned his back on his duty and turned
his back on God. He took ship for Tarshish and went
to sleep. Surely his situation is critical indeed. But
though he has forgotten God, God in His mercy has
not forgotten him. God still loves Jonah, still longs
for him and still hopes for him. And so in mercy
He sends a storm after him. That was dangerous cargo
that that ship had on board. It had better have had
gasoline or T N T than a rebellious prophet.

It was in mercy, I say, that the Lord sent the storm

after Jonah. Coverdale translates it, "The Lord hurled a storm into the sea." Let us thank God for the storms that rouse us, that wake us up, that keep us from sleeping our way into the pit. May the Lord send us any kind of storm rather than allow us to fling ourselves eternally away from His presence. I am so glad God will never allow a man to go comfortably and peacefully to eternal death. He never allows any man to be lost until He has done His best to save him.

I read some years ago of a New England farmer who was driving to town on a cold winter's day. He overtook a woman on the way who was walking and carrying a baby in her arms. He took her up on the seat beside him. The cold became more bitter. He noticed after a while that the woman replied to his questions drowsily. A little later he saw that she was asleep. He knew that unless awakened she would sleep the sleep of death. So he did what at first seemed a cruel thing. He sprang from the wagon, dragged her out into the snow and took the child from her clinging arms. With the child he sprang into the wagon and started his team down the road at a trot. The woman roused herself and began to totter feebly forward. A little later she quickened her pace. At last she broke into a run. And as she caught up with the wagon a little later and the farmer put the baby back into her arms, life had come back to the mother. A temporal loss was a blessing to this woman. Let us thank God for any losses that may come to us that will keep us from sleeping our way to ruin.

So Jonah was down in the sides of the boat asleep. Meanwhile the tempest was raging. Meanwhile the fear-filled crew was rubbing elbows with death. Then a hand is clapped on Jonah's shoulder and he is being given a vigorous shaking and a voice is calling to him. And though it is a heathen voice it is full of rebuke. "What meanest thou, O sleeper? How is it that you can sleep amidst all the agony, amidst all the danger that is about us? When the situation is as it is, how is it that you are not on your knees? Rise and call upon thy God."

I wish through this message that I might take some of you who are sleeping so soundly and peacefully and shake you awake. I wish that God might speak through my voice to my heart and yours and say to us, "What meanest thou, O sleeper? What do you mean by sitting idly and stupidly in the House of God Sunday after Sunday and never doing anything? What do you mean by having children growing up about you and not being enough interested in their spiritual welfare to even have a family altar? How is it that amidst the tremendous issues of moral life and moral death that you can be as complacent and as undisturbed as the dead? Why in the name of all that is reasonable will you continue to 'lie like huge stones across the mouth of the sepulcher where God is trying to raise some Lazarus from the dead?' "

That shake and that message got Jonah awake. He sprang out of his berth and rushed upon the deck. And the sight that met him there made a new man out of him. It changed him from a provincial Jew into a world citizen and a missionary. What did he realize as he looked into the pallid faces of those death threatened men about him? He forgot all about their being heathen. He only remembered that they were one with himself in their common danger and their common need. They were all threatened with death. They all needed somebody to save. And, men and women, that

is true still. We folks differ in many respects, but we
are all alike in this: We have all sinned and we all
need a Savior.

He not only saw that they were one in their needs
but that they were also one in their hopes. He realized
what we have been so long in realizing, and that is
the oneness of the race. He came to know, even in
that distant day, that since we are one body, one
member could not suffer without all members suffering
with it. He faced the fact that his own wicked rebellion against God had not only brought wretchedness
upon himself, but that it was bringing it upon all that
sailed with him. No man ever flees from duty without
incalculable hurt, not only to himself, but to others as
well.

But, thank God, the reverse is also true. If my disobedience hurts my obedience helps. If my sin carries
a curse my righteousness brings a blessing. Here is
another vessel lashed by a tempest. But the preacher
on board this time is on good terms with his God.
Therefore he puts one hand into the hand of his Lord
and with the other he saves the whole company of two
hundred and seventy-six souls that sail with him. "Be
of good cheer: for there shall be no loss of any man's
life among you, but of the ship. For there stood by
me this night the angel of God, whose I am, and whom
I serve, Saying, Fear not, Paul; thou must be brought
before Cæsar: and, lo, God hath given thee all them
that sail with thee."

"How may the sea become calm for us," is the
question. Jonah does not offer an easy suggestion.
"Cast me overboard," is the reply. The man who a
few days ago despised the heathen is now ready to
die for them. That shows that God had made him

a new man. I know he backslides a bit later, but he comes out all right in the end.

And, my brethren, God has no other method for stilling seas than that employed by Jonah. When the tempest of this world's sin was to be stilled there was no cheaper way than for Christ to allow himself to be thrown overboard. When Livingstone wanted to still the tempest of Africa he did not undertake the task from long distance. He allowed himself to be thrown overboard. And that is the price you and I have to pay for real service. "Except a corn of wheat fall into the ground and die, it abideth alone; but if it die, it bringeth forth much fruit."

So Jonah was cast into the sea. But by losing his life he found it. A friend of mine told recently of an experience of his in dealing with a British soldier in India. This soldier was seeking salvation. They prayed together. But as they were about to separate, the soldier was not satisfied. He staggered against the wall and prayed after this fashion: "Lord, my sins are many. I am unworthy of thy salvation. I am unworthy of a vision of thy face. But if there is any place that you want some man to die for you I would count it as a great favor if you would let me be that man." "And then suddenly," said my friend, "the light came into his face and he was conscious of the presence of Christ."

If you will do this to-day, stop running from God and turn and walk with Him, you will find that Nineveh is not a city of restlessness and wretchedness. But you will find that it is a city rich in fellowship with God and in the blessed experience of that peace that passeth all understanding. Which way are you going to travel from this hour? Out of that door you will go in a moment facing toward Nineveh or toward Tarshish. Which way will you face? May God grant that every step you take from this hour may be toward Nineveh.

III

THE ROMANCE OF FAITH—PETER

Matthew 14:28

"Lord, if it be thou, bid me come unto thee on the water." I could not tell you how many times I have read this fascinating story. I have turned to it again and again. But in spite of its familiarity it always grips me. I can never read it thoughtfully without a thrill. I can never expose my soul to the vital truth of it without being helped and made a little bit more hopeful and I trust a little bit better.

Look at the picture. Here is a little ship in the midst of a storm at sea. A dozen men are manning the oars, battling with the tempest, fighting through the long hours of the night with the storm-whipped sea, fisticuffing with death, and yet getting nowhere. It has been long hours since they left the shore. It is now three o'clock in the morning, but they have made very little progress.

I have a fancy that they have become very tired and very discouraged. And more than once has one said to the other, "I wish the Master were here. If He were here He would know what to do." And then, to add to their terror, they suddenly see their Master walking from wave to wave toward them across the sea. But he is not recognized. They take him for a ghost and they cry out in fear.

This is not an altogether unique experience. Many times Jesus comes to us in a way that makes us rather dread than welcome His approach. Sometimes He comes with demands for the giving up of certain sins or certain pleasures that we do not wish to give up. Sometimes He asks us for services that we do not wish to render. He demands surrenders that we do not at all desire to make. Sometimes He comes to us in the guise of a great disappointment. He comes in the garb of a heartache that wets our faces with tears.

The disciples, I say, were at first afraid. But Jesus calmed their fears by saying, "It is I. Be not afraid." The Bible seems to have been written in large measure just to still the fears of our timid hearts. Over and over again is that message directed to us, "Fear not." And at once fear was driven from these hearts. And in the place of fear came, to one at least, a glorious and buoyant faith.

"Lord, if it be thou," shouted Peter, "bid me come to thee on the water." You see the effect the presence of Christ had upon Peter. As soon as he recognized Jesus he ceased to fear and began to hope. As soon as he realized the presence of Christ he gave up doubt and despair and began to believe. The presence of Christ always makes for faith. Peter was gripped by a firm conviction that now that Christ had come impossibilities were transmuted into possibilities.

"Bid me come to thee on the water." Peter had no disposition to climb out of that boat before Jesus came. He had no desire to undertake this seemingly mad task while Christ was yonder on the mountain side and the little boat was being battered by the storm. But Christ had begotten within him a beautiful and seemingly utterly reckless faith. That which a moment ago was an impossibility is now altogether capable of being accomplished.

Christ always inspires such faith in the hearts of those who really know Him. In such faith He takes the keenest delight. There is nothing that so pleases Him as the most daring and reckless and romantic faith. He is never so joyed as when men trust Him with mad abandon. Never once did He praise a prudent and conservative faith. All His encomiums are for those who trust Him with a romantic recklessness.

Did you happen to meet the woman with the issue of blood as she set out to see Jesus? Well, it is good that you did not or you would have done your best to have discouraged her. Of course you would and so would I. "Sarah," I would have said, "are you going to ask Jesus to help you? Are you going to seek him out and fall on your face before Him in prayer?" "No," she would have answered, "I am not going to pray. I am not going to ask the Master to do anything for me at all. I am simply going to slip up behind Him when the crowd is thronging Him, and touch His garment. I have a shamefaced disease. I want as little attention as possible. Hence I am not going to say a single word to Jesus."

Then, I would have answered with conviction, "You will never be cured. The Master has made no promise that He will honor a mad faith like yours. When did He say He would heal if you merely slipped up in a mob and touched the fringe of His garment?" But I was not there to throw dashes of cold water upon the fire. She went on her reckless way. And wonder of wonders, she was healed.

"Lord, bid me come," said Peter. And what was the reply of Jesus? Did He say, "Peter, I am astonished at you. Why do you want to do this foolish and insane and impossible thing? Don't you know that the storm is against you? Don't you know that the law of gravitation is against you? Don't you know that the whole experience of the race is against you? You have been about the sea all your life. When did you ever see anybody walk on the waves? Why do you request, then, to do this absurd and ridiculous and impossible thing?"

But Jesus did not say that. I never read where He told a single trusting heart that his request was impossible. I do read where He said the very opposite. He said, "All things are possible to him that believeth." He makes all things possible. That is what he is for. He ever attacks men at the point of their impossibilities. He calls on the selfish man to love his neighbor as himself. He calls on the paralytics to rise and walk. And never does He have a rebuke for the man who dares to fling himself blindly upon His power.

And instead of rebuking Peter He approved him. He encouraged him. He set His sanction upon his request. He said to him, "Come." I am sure if you or I had been there we would have wanted Him to have said far more. We would have wanted Him to explain to us how He would hold us and enable us to walk. But the invitation, "Come," that one word was enough for Peter.

"Come," said Jesus. What would you have done under those circumstances? What would I? I suppose I know. I would have said, "Lord, I'd like to. I wish I could. I've always wanted to do something magnificent. It has occurred to me again and again as I have read the record of thy dealings with thy saints that the Christian life is not to be a dull and drab and unromantic thing. I have felt a thousand times that the faith of the saints ought to have far more of buoyancy and enthusiasm and daring and romantic adventure in it than it has. So since you have bid me come, Lord, I'd like to come. I'll think it over. Who knows but that I may try it some day?"

But Peter was made out of more heroic stuff. The spirit of adventure had not died within him. His faith is full of the finest romance. "Come," said Jesus and immediately I see Peter drop his oar and begin to climb down out of the boat to go to Jesus.

Some of the commentators are very hard on Peter for his boldness and seeming foolhardiness here. But I am frank to say that I like Peter here very much. I suppose most of the critics would have sat very still in the boat. I shouldn't wonder if they would not have put a restraining hand upon Peter. In fact, it would not surprise me if some of his fellow disciples did not do that very thing. I can imagine that Andrew might have gripped him and said, "Peter, sit where you are. You can hardly stay on top of the water now." And Thomas would have said, "Man, are you mad? Nobody ever walked on the water before." But Peter said, "By the help of Christ I will." And with the "storm light in his face" and the spray in his hair and with faith in Christ in his heart he pushes the boat from under his feet.

There is something great about that. There may be much base alloy in Peter, but there is something fine in him also. He is to be admired if he never takes a step. He is worthy of praise if he sinks into the sea as a piece of lead. At least he has dreamed of doing the supernatural. At least he has dared in the presence of Christ to undertake what others were afraid to undertake. He has ventured to stake his life on the power of Christ to make good His promise. If he fails utterly he is still worthy of respect. It is better to make a thousand failures than to be too cowardly to ever undertake anything.

So he steps out upon a stormy sea. It does look a bit mad, doesn't it? And yet it only looks mad because of our blindness and dullness and stupid unbelief. What did Peter have under him when he was in the ship? Upon what were his fellow disciples trusting to keep them from the bottom of the sea? Just two or three planks, that is all. Upon what was Peter trusting? He was trusting upon the sure word of God. When he let himself down from the side of the boat at Christ's invitation he did not drop into the sea. He dropped into God's arms. He dropped into the arms of Him who holds every sea in the hollow of His hand. He dropped into the arms of Him whose power kindled every sun and flung every world into space. Before Peter can sink he must break God's arm. And mad as seemed his act Peter was never so safe in his life. Pile upon him, if you will, all the mountain systems of all the worlds and he will never sink low enough to wet his sandals if he keeps his feet planted upon the promise of Christ.

Jesus said, "Come." Peter did the same that you and I may do. He responded in the affirmative. He said, "Yes, Lord," and made the venture. And what happened? Let me read it to you. "He walked on the water to go to Jesus." He did what was humanly impossible. He accomplished what was absolutely beyond the reach of any human being except for the power of Christ. He walked. It must have been a thrilling experience. It was a joy to himself. It was a joy to his Master. It was a benediction to his fellows. I can see the terror in their faces give way to wonderment and gladness as they say, "Well, well, well! He is doing it after all."

Yes, Peter walked. Let us not let any subsequent failure blind us to this blessed fact. I know that he did not walk far. I know, too, that that was his own fault. It was not the fault of his Lord. Peter might have walked the whole distance but for one fatal mistake. He might have won a complete triumph but for one tragic loss.

What happened to Peter? "He saw the wind boisterous." What does this mean? It means that Peter ceased giving his attention and his confidence to Christ. He fixed upon the difficulties. In other words, he lost his faith. He came to believe in his hindrances more than in his help. He believed in Christ a great deal, but he believed more in waves and wind and lightning and thunder. He believed in Jesus, but he believed more in weakness and death. Looking at the wind he stepped right off God's promise and it wasn't a second till he was up to his neck in the raging water.

There was absolutely no failure possible so long as he stood firm upon the promise of Christ. "Come unto me, all ye that labor and are heavy laden," Jesus is saying to you that are troubled and sin burdened. That means that you can come. That means that He is eager for you to come. And however far you have gone from God and however stiff may be the tempest that blows about you, if you get this promise under your feet all the storms that hell can let loose against a human soul will leave you unshaken. But you must keep a firm stand on the promise.

If you are here with some great yearning in

your heart, some special prayer for usefulness or
for deliverance from a peculiar temptation, lay hold on
God's Word and cling to it and you will never be put
to confusion. A saintly old friend of mine told me
on one occasion about praying for his child. And he
said he got the assurance that his baby was going to
recover. She was suffering from membranous croup.
That very night he was awakened by the mother and
the nurse. And he heard the mother say to the nurse,
"Is she dead?" And he turned and went to sleep with
never a question and never a doubt. He refused to
look at the waves.

Peter got too interested and too absorbed in difficulties. It is so easy to do that. Peter took counsel of
his fears. I have done the same and you have done
the same a thousand times over. We are not going
to be harsh and critical with him. By so doing we
would be too hard upon ourselves. But this I say: It
is a great calamity. It is a great shame. Oh, that
we might get upon the higher ground of the psalmist
who said, "Wherefore will we not fear though the
earth be removed and though the mountains be cast into
the midst of the sea."

But looking at the boisterous wind and taking counsel
of our fears,—these are not the only things that work
our ruin. We might be persuaded, and often are,
to take our eyes off Christ as much by our advantages
as by our disadvantages. Had Peter said within himself, "The law of gravitation is not so invariable as I
thought," or "I am a much superior man to what I
dreamed I was." If Peter had fixed his confidence in
self or in circumstances he would have gone down just
the same. Anything that turns our eyes away from a
steadfast gaze of faith upon Christ spells disaster.

What happened to Peter when he began to look at the boisterous wind? You know. He began to sink. Peter sinking right in the presence of Christ,—that is pathetic. He can help nobody now. He could not have saved his own child if he had been there. Unbelievers seated smugly in the boat said, "Ah! I thought so. I knew something like that would happen." I do not know that Peter would ever have noticed the boisterous wind unless somebody had called his attention to it. I can imagine Thomas might have shouted to Peter and said, "Look out, Peter. There comes a tremendous wave." Anyway, Peter is sinking.

Did you ever have that experience? Do you know what it is to feel that soul sickening sensation that comes to one who is sinking? Do you know what it means to be losing your grip on God, losing your power in prayer, losing your grip of things spiritual? Did you ever sink? Are you sinking to-day? I think I know something of the experience of Peter. I have an idea that you know something of it.

Young man, away from home for the first time, are you sinking? Little by little are you giving up your faith? Little by little are you flinging away the fine ideals that were the strength of your earlier years? Young woman, are you sinking? Business man, cumbered with many cares, living your life in the thick of the fight, are you keeping straight and clean or are you losing your vision? Are you sinking? What was the matter with Lot in Sodom? He led a sinking life. That was it and it cost him every one that was dear to him. It will prove expensive to you. Oh, Christian worker, you will not count as long as you are living a defeated and failing and sinking life.

But even in his failure Peter has a message for us.

In his defeat he is his own straightforward, sincere and honest self. When Peter realized that he was sinking he did not try to conceal the matter. He did not say, "I'll fight it out in my own strength." He threw himself at once on the infinite strength of Christ. He prayed. That was a wise thing. That was a big and manly thing. Peter prayed. Have you forgotten the art?

And listen to that prayer. It was white hot with earnestness. "Lord, save me." It is short, too. Notice that. When you do not want anything, when you have no burden, when you are careless and indifferent and listless, you can get down on your knees and pour out whole hogsheads of mere words. When you are spiritually asleep and morally stupid you can utter platitudes in the form of prayer endlessly. But when the sword of genuine conviction has passed through your soul, when you are doing business in great waters, then you fling aside your platitudinous petitions and call out in solemn earnestness for help.

That prayer was a confession. It was a confession of failure, a confession of defeat. It was also a confession of need. Some men would have been too proud to have made it. What a terrible thing is pride, that damning pride that makes us unwilling to confess our sin even to God. "For he that covereth his sin shall not prosper." But "if we confess our sins, He is faithful and just to forgive us our sins and to cleanse us from all unrighteousness."

Peter was different. That was his salvation. He blurted out the whole pitiful story and threw himself on the mercy of Jesus. And what happened? That which always happens when men thus pray. "Immediately Jesus stretched forth His hand and caught him." And Peter, who had walked and had sunk, rose and walked again. And so may you and so may every single sinking and floundering and failing soul here. All you need to do is pray as Peter prayed and to believe as Peter believed.

And now, my brethren, do you not agree that we need more of the faith that made Peter undertake his mad enterprise? Isn't the tragedy of the Church to-day just this, that the average Christian is not walking by faith, but by sight? That is the reason we have so little of that high spirit of daring that marked the early Church. That is the reason that life for many of us is so dull and prosaic. What we need is faith. For faith is not a tame and spineless thing that dares nothing. Real faith dares something, something big and brawny, beyond the human. Hence it brings into life the thrill of finest romance.

"Come," said Jesus, and Peter gave an instant obedience. May you and I be as wise. For our Lord is inviting us just as He invited Peter. Are you thirsty? He says, "Come to me and drink." Are you hungry? He says, "Come and dine." Are you tired and burdened? He says, "Come and I will give you rest." Are you eager to be of service? He says, "Come,—and out of your inner life shall flow rivers of living water." Brethren, all our needs are met in Him. He is our sufficiency. He is summoning us even now to venture upon Him. "Will you make the venture?

> "Out of my shameful failure and loss,
>   Jesus, I come, Jesus, I come;
> Into the glorious gain of Thy cross,
>   Jesus, I come to Thee;
> Out of the depths of ruin untold,
> Into the peace of Thy sheltering fold,
> Ever hereafter Thy face to behold,
>   Jesus, I come to Thee."

IV

LOVE'S LONGING—PAUL

Philippians 3 : 10

"That I may know . . . the fellowship of His sufferings." Weymouth gives this translation: "I long to share His sufferings." Paul is here leading, us into the very innermost sanctuary of his heart. He is revealing to us the supreme passion of his life. He is letting us know what is his one great ambition. "I long," he says. And knowing what a mighty man he was we lean eagerly forward that we may hear the word that comes from his lips. For we are keen to know what is the dearest desire of this brave heart.

And as we listen this is the perplexing word that comes to us: "I long to share in His sufferings." How startlingly strange that longing is. We are half ready to wonder if we have heard aright. And when we realize that we have, we instinctively think of the words of the Roman governor, Festus: "Paul, thou art beside thyself. Much learning doth make thee mad." We wonder if Festus was not right after all. Isn't Paul a bit insane?

"I long to share in His suffering." It sounds like madness to many of us because it is so foreign to our own deepest desires. Had Paul said, "I long for a place of honor; I long that my presence should elicit the applause of the world and call forth the crowns of the world"; had he said this, we could easily have understood him. Had he expressed a longing for a place

46

in the hall of fame, had he said, "My one desire is that the world shall keep sacred my memory," he would have been easily understood by us. We would have said, "This is very natural and very human." But that is not what he says. This is his strange language: "I long to share in Christ's sufferings."

Had Paul said that he longed to escape pain and anguish and sorrow we might also have understood him. Had he said, "I long to escape the penalty of sin even though I live in sin," many of us could have appreciated this desire. For there are always those who, while they do not yearn especially for deliverance from sin, do yearn to be saved from its penalty. They do not desire to be saved from the sowing of tares, but they want to be saved from the reaping of the harvest. They do not pray for deliverance from the broad road, but they desire that this broad road terminate at the gate of Heaven instead of at the gate of destruction. Had this man said that he desired to escape hell everybody could have sympathized with him. But that is not his desire.

What he said was entirely different. "I long," he says, "to share in the sufferings of Christ; I long to weep as He wept; I long to sympathize as He sympathized; I long to travel life by His road; I long to pass through His Gethsemane and to climb His Calvary and to share in my finite way in His Cross." It is an amazing desire. What is its secret?

Why could Paul truly say such a word as this? In the first place, he could not say it because it was natural for him. There had been a time when if he had given utterance to such a statement it would have been grossly false. When Paul rode out from Jerusalem on his way to Damascus, for instance, he

longed for anything else more than he longed
to share in the sufferings of Christ. It required
a marvelous change. It required an absolute transfor-
mation to bring Paul to the place where he was able
to give utterance to this high and heroic sentiment.
He was not possessed of such a longing by nature.

Nor did Paul long to share in the sufferings of
Christ because he looked upon these sufferings as trivial.
Few men have ever understood the sufferings of Christ
as did Paul. He had an appreciation of their intensity
and of their bitterness far beyond most other men. He
understood as few have ever understood the physical
agonies of the Cross. Paul was a great physical sufferer himself.

But he knew what we sometimes forget, that infinitely
the deepest pain of Jesus was not physical. Had there
been nothing involved in His crucifixion but physical
agony then we are forced to acknowledge that many of
His followers have endured the same kind of pain
with a fortitude to which He was a stranger. His
agony was from another source. He suffered because
He was made "to be sin for us, who knew no sin."
He suffered in that "he was wounded for our transgressions and bruised for our iniquities." It was this
fact that wrung from Him that bitterest of all cries,
"My God, my God, why hast thou forsaken me?"

Nor did Paul possess this desire because he longed
for pain in itself. Paul was not a calloused soul.
Few men have ever been more sensitive to pain.
He had no more fondness for being shipwrecked than
you and I have. He had no more pleasure in being
stoned, in being publicly whipped, in being thrown into
dark dungeons and stenchful prison cells than you and
I have. He no more delighted in being ridiculed and

ostracized than you and I would delight in these things. Paul took no more pleasure in hunger and cold, in peril and nakedness, in agony and tears than you and I would take in them.

Yet we find him longing to share in the sufferings of Christ. Why did he long for this strange privilege? There are two reasons. He longed to share in Christ's sufferings, first, because he genuinely and passionately loved Christ. If you have ever at any time truly loved anybody you will be able to understand this longing of Saint Paul. It is the nature of love to always seek either to spare or to share the pain of the loved one.

One of the sweetest stories in our American literature, I think, is that of "The Wife" told by Washington Irving. You remember it. It has been re-enacted a thousand times over. A man of wealth has lost his fortune. He is heart-broken over it, not on his own account but on account of his wife. She has been tenderly nurtured. He is sure that poverty will break her heart. But he has to tell her. The lovely home in the city must be given up. They must move to a cottage in the country. He enters upon the hard ordeal. It is his Gethsemane. But to his utter amazement he finds his wife more joyous, more genuinely happy in the midst of this trying experience than he has ever known her to be before. What is the secret? She is in love with her husband and loving him, it is her keenest joy to be able to share his sorrow with him.

The wife of the southern poet, Sidney Lanier, was just such a one as Irving's heroine. You will recall what a long hard fight Lanier had with sickness and poverty and what a tower of strength through it all was the gentle and tender woman who loved him.

"In the heart of the Hills of Life, I know
Two springs that with unbroken flow
Forever pour their lucent streams
Into my soul's far Lake of Dreams.

Not larger than two eyes, they lie,
Beneath the many-changing sky
And mirror all of life and time,
—Serene and dainty pantomime.

Shot through with lights of stars and dawns,
And shadowed sweet by ferns and fawns,
—Thus heaven and earth together vie
Their shining depth to sanctify.

Always when the large Form of Love
Is hid by storms that rage above,
I gaze in my two springs and see
Love in his very verity.
            .   .   .   .

O Love, O Wife, thine eyes are they,
—My springs from out whose shining gray
Issue the sweet celestial streams
That feed my life's bright Lake of Dreams.

Oval and large and passion-pure
And gray and wise and honor-sure;
Soft as a dying violet-breath
Yet calmly unafraid of death.
            .   .   .   .

Dear eyes, dear eyes and rare complete—
Being heavenly-sweet and earthly-sweet,
—I marvel that God made you mine,
For when He frowns, 'tis then ye shine!"

Now, what was there in the seeming frown of God to
make the eyes of love shine? It was just this: they
were alight with the joy that comes when love is privileged to share the pain of the beloved.

I heard a grizzled old soldier who was an officer in

the Civil War tell of a raw recruit who came into his
regiment. This recruit was awkward and uncouth and
unattractive. He seemed to be little more than an incarnate blunder. He would stumble and fall down over
his own musket. Naturally he was the butt of many
jokes. He was the laughing stock of all his comrades.
But this officer said that he tried to befriend him.
But if the uncouth fellow appreciated his efforts to
help him he never said so. He seemed as awkward
in expressing himself as he was in all other respects.

"One night," said this officer, "we were sleeping
without tents and it was bitter cold. I shivered under
my blanket till I went to sleep. When I waked in the
morning, however, I was warm. Then I noticed, to
my astonishment, that I was sleeping under two blan-
kets instead of one. I looked about me for an expla-
nation. A little way off was this gawky, green, uncouth
soldier striding back and forth with the snow pelting
him in the face. He was waving his thin arms as he
walked to keep from freezing to death. That soldier
died a few days later. He died from the exposure of
that night. But a smile was on his face as I sat beside
him." Now, why did the soldier smile? You know.
He was rejoicing that he was able to spare and to share
the suffering of his friend.

"I long to share in His sufferings." That is the
language of love. To one who does not know love
it will forever be a mystery. But to the lover it is easily
comprehensible. Any real mother can understand it.
Down in Tennessee a few years ago a mother was out
riding with her little boy. The horse took fright and
ran away. The buggy was wrecked. The mother escaped without injury. But the little lad was so crippled that he was never able to sit up again.

Now, before this tragic accident the mother of this little wounded boy had been very active in the life of her Church and community. But with the coming of this great sorrow she had to give up all outside work. She gave herself instead night and day to the nursing of her boy. At times she would hold the little fellow in her arms for almost the whole night through. At last, after three years, the angel of release came and the patient sufferer went home. And there were those in the community who said, "I know that his mother will grieve. Yet his home-going must be a bit of a relief."

But what said the mother when the minister went to see her? She met the preacher at the door and as love's sweet rain ran down her face she did not say anything about being relieved at all. But this is what she said: "Oh, Brother, my little boy is gone and I can't get to do anything for him any more." Why, it was the grief of her heart that the little fellow had gone out beyond the reach of her hand where she could no longer have the joy of offering herself a living sacrifice upon the altar of his need. She longed to continually share in his suffering.

So Paul wanted to share in the sufferings of Christ because he loved Christ. Then he wanted to share in the sufferings of Christ, in the second place, because he knew that suffering was involved in being like Christ. You may suffer and yet be un-Christlike, but no man can be Christlike and fail to suffer. If you ever, by the grace of God, become a partaker of the divine nature you must also inevitably become a partaker of His sufferings.

To be Christlike is to suffer for the very simple reason that Christ cannot be what He is and fail to suffer in and for a world like ours. What is the nature of Christ? Christ is like God. Christ is God. "He that hath seen me hath seen the Father." But what is God? There are many definitions. There is only one all comprehensive and all inclusive definition. That is that sentence of pure gold that fell from the lips of the apostle that leaned upon the bosom of his Lord. "What is God?" I ask this man who had such a wonderful knowledge of Him. And he answers, "God is love."

Now since God is love He must suffer. He cannot look upon the lost and ruined of this world without grief. He cannot behold the tragic quarrel of man with Himself without taking it to heart. There is nothing more true nor, in the deepest sense, more reasonable than this tender sentence: "In all their afflictions He was afflicted." Our afflictions must afflict Him because "His nature and His name is love."

J. Wilbur Chapman tells how he one night explored the slums of New York with Sam Hadley. About one o'clock in the morning they separated to go to their own homes. Dr. Chapman said he had not gone far before he heard Mr. Hadley saying, "Oh! Oh! Oh!" And he looked back to see his friend wringing his hands in deepest agony. He hurried to his side thinking that he had been taken suddenly ill. "What is the matter?" he asked. And the great mission worker turned his pain-pinched face back toward the slums out of which they had come and said, "Oh, the sin! Oh, the heartache! Oh, the wretchedness! It will break my heart. It has broken my heart."

Now, just as Christ cannot be Christ and not suffer in a world like ours, so He cannot be Himself and fail to make a sacrificial effort to save this world. What says the gem of the Gospel? "God so loved the world that He gave." What was the song that abidingly made Paul's heart to pulsate with heavenly hallelujahs? Just this: "He loved me and gave Himself for me." Love grieves. It does more. It serves. Love beholds the city and weeps over it. But it is not satisfied with that. It also goes to the Cross for that city over which it weeps. Sam Hadley wrings his hands in grief over the wretched in New York's slums, but he does more. He goes to their rescue.

So when Paul said, "I long to share His sufferings" he meant, "I long to be, in the truest sense, like Him. I long to see the world through His eyes. I long to feel toward men as Christ feels toward them. I long to sacrifice for them in my finite way as He sacrificed for them." And what was the outcome of this longing? There are some ambitions that God cannot gratify. To do so would only mean our impoverishment and our ruin. But such is not the case here. God graciously granted the satisfying of this longing of Saint Paul.

Listen to the testimony to the truth of that fact from his own lips. "I am crucified with Christ, nevertheless I live. Yet not I, but Christ liveth in me." Again he says, "For to me to live is Christ." That is, "For to me to live is to reproduce Christ. For to me to live is for Christ to live over again in me." In a most profound and vital sense he has come to share in the divine nature.

Having come to share in the divine nature he is privileged also to share in His sufferings. His ministry is a daily dying. He is a man of great heaviness and continual sorrow. The secret of his pain is this: "I fill up that which is behind of the sufferings of Christ in my body." In sharing thus his Master's sufferings he shared with him in His work of bringing salvation to men. To-day we could better spare many a nation than we could spare this one single man.

And now we are going to gather about this altar where we shall remember together the suffering love of Jesus Christ. As we take the bread and wine we are going to be reminded of the broken body and shed blood of our Lord. And I trust that as we think upon His love and upon His sacrifice for ourselves we shall come to be possessed with the holy longing of this great apostle. May we too be able to say, "I long to share in His suffering." This high longing is possible for every one of us through the riches of His grace. And it is possible in no other way. Therefore, let us gather round this table with this song within our hearts:

"Thy nature, gracious Lord, impart;
  Come quickly from above,
Write thy new name upon my heart,
  Thy new, best name of Love."

V

GOING VISITING—JONATHAN

I Samuel 23 : 16

"And Jonathan, Saul's son, arose and went to David into the wood and strengthened his hand in God." "Going visiting" is a very commonplace occurrence. Oftentimes the visits we make are thoroughly trivial and unimportant. But there are other times when our visits take on a profound significance. There are times when they mark a crisis. There are times when they set in motion influences that tell on the entire future of those whom we visit. There are times when they mean the making or the marring of a human soul.

Now, this visit about which we are to study to-day is no ordinary visit. I think it is one of the most beautiful stories to be found in literature. This visit was made many centuries ago. It was made in an obscure corner of the earth, and yet it has never been forgotten. It never will be. The Inspirer of the Word saw in it too much of worth and winsomeness to allow it to slip out of the memories of men. It is remembered to-day, not because Jonathan left his calling card on David's center table. It is remembered because the visit was so blessedly beautiful.

It is a great privilege that God has given us in allowing us to visit each other. We can help so much by it if we will. Wasn't that a lovely visit that the old school master made to Marget that time in "Beside the Bonny Briar Bush" when he came to tell her that

56

she had a "laddie of parts"? And wasn't it still more
beautiful when he came later, rugged old Scotchman
that he was, to burst into tears of wild joy over the
good news he brought her that her son had won first
prize in the great university?

Wasn't that a lovely series of visits that a kindly
old man made to the room of the little laddie who
had swept the street crossing before he had been crippled in the discharge of his duty? A city missionary
went in to see him and asked him if he had had
anybody to visit him. "Oh, yes," was the answer.
"A good man comes every day and talks to me, and
sometimes he reads the Bible to me and prays." "What
is his name?" asked the missionary. And the little
fellow studied a moment and said, "I think he said
his name was Gladstone." England's grand old man
appears to us in many a charming rôle, but in none
is he more manly and commanding than in this of
visiting a little crippled waif in a London attic.

Florence Nightingale was a lovely visitor. Do you
recall that exquisite bit of poetry in conduct on the
field of Crimea? A soldier was to go through a painful operation. An anæsthetic could not be adminis-
tered and the doctor said the patient could not endure
the operation. "Yes, I can," said the patient, "under
one condition: if you will get the 'Angel of the Crimea'
to hold my hand." And she came out to the little
hospital at the front and held his hand. Glorious visit.
No wonder the man went through the operation without a tremor.

But the visit of our text,—to me it is more wonderful still. The truth of the matter is, I know of but
one other visit that ever took place that is finer and
more beautiful. You know what visit that was. It

was the visit that ONE made to a manger in Bethlehem
nineteen centuries ago. That was a visit that remade
the world. It was so wonderful that a star pointed
it out with finger of silver, and our discordant old
earth was serenaded with the music of that land of
eternal melody. But aside from that one visit, I think
this the most beautiful one ever recorded.

What is the secret of its beauty? First, it was
beautiful in its courageous loyalty. You know who
Jonathan was. He was the King's son. He was popular, handsome and courageous. So lithe, athletic and
graceful he was that they called him "the gazelle."
He was a prince. He was heir-apparent to the throne
of Israel.

And you know, also, who David was. He was at
that time in disgrace. He was under the frown of
the King. He was being hunted from one refuge to
another like a wild beast. To be his friend was to
be the enemy of the King. To smile upon him was to
meet the frown of the King.

But notwithstanding the fact that these men were
so far apart, one a favorite prince and the other an
outcast peasant, yet we find the prince visiting the
peasant. You say they were friends. Yes, that is true,
deeply true. But their friendship had started in other
days. When David and Jonathan first met they met
under altogether different circumstances. You know
when Jonathan first saw David. It was when David
returned from his fight with Goliath, with the bloody
head of the giant in his hand. He met him amidst
the hurrahs and the wild enthusiasm of the people.
He met him on one of the great red letter days of
David's life, when he sprang suddenly from obscurity
to be a national hero.

It does not seem so surprising, therefore, when we read that on this day "the soul of Jonathan was knit to the soul of David." David was courageous. David had shown himself a hero. David was a favorite with the King and a favorite with the people. It took no great effort to love him then. It took no great courage to be his friend. But all is changed now. The King no longer loves him, but hates him and seeks his life. The sun of his popularity has gone into eclipse. We wonder if Jonathan's friendship will stand the test.

And again we turn and read the text: "And Jonathan, Saul's son, arose and went to David into the wood and strengthened his hand in God." What beautiful loyalty. What fine fidelity. How blessed is David in the friendship of a man who can love him in the sunshine and who can love him no less in the midst of the shadows. How blessed he is in the friendship of one who can stand by him when many lips praise him and who can also stand by him when many abuse him, and many criticise him and many lift their hands against him. Truly this man loves David for himself alone.

Second, this visit is beautiful because of its fine and costly sympathy. Jonathan really sympathized with David in his trials and his difficulties. He did not express that sympathy in any cheap and distant way. He might have sent David word that if he needed anything just to let him know. He might have dispatched a servant to comfort David in his sore trials. But he did not try to express his sympathy at long distance. He went to David. He came to handclasp with the man that he wished to help.

Now, I am perfectly aware of the fact that much of our sympathy must be expressed at a distance. For instance, we cannot all go to the foreign field. We must express our interest in those who have not had our opportunities by our gifts. Much of the service we render in our own land must be rendered in the same way. But when that is said, the fact still remains that there is nothing that will take the place of our hand-to-hand dealing with those who need us. We cannot perform all our charities by proxy. We must come in personal contact with those whom we would help.

There is one poem I think that we have a bit overworked:

"Let me live in my house by the side of the road,
　Where the race of men go by.
They are good, they are bad, they are weak, they are strong,
　Wise, foolish—and so am I.
So why should I sit in the scorner's seat,
　Or hurl the cynic's ban?
Let me live in my house by the side of the road,
　And be a friend to man.

"I see from my house by the side of the road,
　By the side of the highway of life,
The men that press on with the ardor of hope,
　And the men who are faint in the strife.
But I turn not away from their smiles nor their tears,
　Both parts of an infinite plan.
Let me live in my house by the side of the road,
　And be a friend to man.

"I know there are brook gladdened meadows ahead,
　And mountains of wearisome height.
And the road passes on through the long afternoon,
　And stretches away to the night.
But still I rejoice when the travelers rejoice,
　And weep with the strangers that moan,
Nor live in my house by the side of the road,
　Like one who dwells alone."

Now that is good, but after all,—

"It's only a half truth the poet has sung
  Of the house by the side of the way.
  Our Master had neither a house nor a home,
  But He walked with the crowd day by day.
  I think when I read of the poet's desire
  That a house by the road would be good,
  But service is found in its tenderest form
  As we walk with the crowd in the road.

"So I say let me walk with the men in the road,
  Let me seek out the burdens that crush;
  Let me speak a kind word of good cheer to the weak
  Who are falling behind in the rush.
  There are wounds to be healed, there are breaks we must
       mend,
  There are cups of cold water to give,
  And the man in the road by the side of his friend,
  Is the man who has learned how to give.

"Then tell me no more of the house by the road,
  There is only one place I can live.
  It is there where the men are toiling along,
  Who are needing the help I can give.
  'Tis pleasant to dwell in the house by the road,
  And be a friend, as the poet has said,
  But the Master is bidding us, Bear ye their load,
  Your rest waiteth yonder ahead.

"So I can not remain in the house by the road,
  And watch as the toilers pass on,
  Their faces beclouded with pain and with shame,
  So burdened, their strength nearly gone.
  I will go to their side, I will speak in good cheer,
  I will help them to carry their load.
  And I'll smile at the man in the house by the way,
  While I walk with the crowd in the road.

"Out there in the road that runs by the house
Where the poet is singing his song,
I'll walk and I'll work midst the heat of the day,
And I'll help falling brothers along.
Too busy to dwell in the house by the way,
Too happy for such an abode,
And my glad heart will sing to the Master of all,
Who is helping me serve in the road."

And the beauty and glory of this lovely visit that
Prince Jonathan made to David, the outcast, was that
he walked with him in the road. He did not dwell
in his princely palace and send him some money. He
did not allow him, as Dives allowed Lazarus, to gather
up the crumbs. He went to him. And because he went
to him he helped him. Oh, heart, that is the secret of
the salvation wrought by our Lord. He came to us.
Had He merely come for the day and gone back to
Heaven at night, He would never have saved us. He
came into personal contact with us. That is how He
lifts us.

This visit was beautiful, in the third place, because
of its high and holy purpose. I see Jonathan as he is
turning his face toward the forest where David is hiding.
I say to him, "Prince Jonathan, you are going down to
see David, I understand. Why are you going?" This
is his answer: "I am going down to strengthen his hand
in God. You know David has had a hard time recently.
He has been sorely tried. He has been bitterly disappointed. He has passed through one great sorrow after
another. I am afraid his faith is going to be destroyed.
I am afraid he will lose his grip of God unless I go to
see him and help him and strengthen his hand in the
Lord. And that is why I am going."

And so Jonathan hurries on. And the angels must

have crowded the windows of heaven to behold him as he walked upon this glorious errand. I would go a bit out of my way any time to get to see a man who is going to see his friend, not to ask for help, but going for the one big purpose of making the man whom he is to visit a little stronger, a little better, a little more loyal to his Lord.

And not only did Jonathan go for that purpose, but he succeeded in it. When he left David, he left him a stronger man. I do not know what he said to him. That is not recorded. I do not know that he quoted scripture to him or even prayed with him. He may have. He may not have. It is not absolutely necessary to have prayer always in order to strengthen our friend in the Lord. Sometimes all we need to do is just to talk to him and let him talk, and convince him that we sympathize with him, that we are interested in him. And having done that, somehow he comes more and more to believe in God's interest.

But whatever Jonathan said, David was stronger and better and braver after he had gone. I think I can hear him as he looks after the retreating figure going through the forest. And what he is saying to himself is this, "Bless the Lord, O my soul, and all that is within me, bless His holy name." And I think when the books are balanced in Heaven that Jonathan will get quite a bit of credit for David's exquisite music. There are terrible clashes in his songs. "He that did eat of my bread hath lifted up his heel against me." Jonathan did not inspire that. But there is many a blessed passage that might never have been written but for the loyal and loving and constant friendship of Prince Jonathan.

And last of all, this visit was beautiful in its self-

forgetfulness. Its beauty reached its climax here. Just
think of the circumstances. Samuel, the prophet, has
declared that David is to be king. But in everybody's
mind, the throne by right belongs to Jonathan. David
is in perplexity. He is on the point of losing his faith.
If he loses it he never will be king. This will give
Jonathan his chance.

Now, why, I wonder, didn't Jonathan feel about this
matter as many of us would? Why did he not hold aloof
and say, "If David fails and loses his chance it is no
fault of mine. If he fails it will only mean that he
will not take away the throne that by right belongs
to me." No attitude would have been more human
than this. I do not know how many nights Jonathan
spent in prayer to be delivered from the bondage of his
selfishness. But I do know this, that he was delivered.

And I want you to watch him as he goes down
into this forest to see David to-day to strengthen his
hand in God. I said we do not know his conversa-
tion with David. We do know a bit of it, and that
is this, that he encouraged David to believe God, to
believe this one particular promise at least, that God
was going to see to it that David was king. And when
you see Jonathan going thus into the woods he is going for the deliberate purpose of taking the crown off
his own brow and putting it upon the brow of another. He is abdicating the throne in behalf of this
outcast friend of his who is hiding here in the forest.

You will doubtless agree, therefore, that this old
world has not been blessed with many visits so beautiful as this. Watch this Prince as he goes into the
wood. His stride is like that of another:—

"Into the woods my Master went,
  Clean forspent, forspent;
Into the woods my Master came,
  Forspent with love and shame.
But the olive trees were not blind to Him,
And the little gray leaves were kind to Him,
And the thorn tree had a mind to Him,
  When into the woods He came.

"Out of the woods my Master went,
  And He was well content;
Out of the woods my Master came,
  Content with death and shame.
When death and shame would woo Him last,
From under the trees they drew Him last,
'Twas on a tree they slew him—last
  When out of the woods He came."

Yes, Jonathan went into the woods to uncrown himself! to empty himself for his friend! Truly "the spirit and mind was in him that was also in Christ Jesus, who being in the form of God thought it not a thing to be clung to to be equal with God, but emptied Himself and became obedient unto death, even the death of the cross."

But the "practical" man stands aside and looks on and says, "Jonathan, you have made a great mistake. You never wore a crown and you never wielded a scepter. You took your opportunity for earthly greatness and threw it away. It was a great mistake." And we take the words of Judas and say, "Why this waste?"

But after all, was it a mistake? He lost his crown, but he won his friend. He helped banish the discord and increased the melody of the world. He threw aside his scepter of temporal power to lay hold on an eternal scepter. He threw aside the crown that he might have worn for a day to lay hold on a crown that will last forever more.

If ever I get to Heaven I expect to give particular attention to the Visitors' Gallery. I think there is going to be an especial place, a very choice place in Heaven for the visitors. Not, you will understand, for those who are visiting Heaven, but those who were good at visiting here. For mark you, the Lord has spoken of a special reward that He is going to give to those of whom He could say, "Ye visited me." And about the handsomest, the loveliest face I expect to find among the immortal and blood-washed visitors is the face of this man Jonathan.

And now, will you hear this closing word? Jonathan uncrowned himself for his friend. And he won his friend and he won an immortal crown. But there was another who gave up infinitely more than Jonathan. And He came to you and me when we were in an infinitely worse plight than that in which David was. He came to us when we were dead in trespasses and in sin. And what He says to us this morning is this, "I have called you friends. Ye are my friends."

The Prince who did that for us was not the son of Saul, but the Son of God. Through His renunciation He was crowned. By His stooping He was forever elevated. "Wherefore God has highly exalted Him and given Him a name that is above every name." But what I ask is this: Have you responded to His friendship as David responded to that of Jonathan? He has been a friend to you. Have you, will you be a friend to Him? That is what He is seeking. That is what He is longing for to-day as for nothing else in earth or Heaven.

You know why He came. You know why He is

here now. Why did Jonathan visit David in the gloomy wood that day and uncrown himself for him? It was just this reason: It was because he loved him. Again and again the story had said that Jonathan loved David as his own soul. I thought it was a mere hyperbole at first. I thought it might be a kind of poetic way of putting it, but it was only sober truth. And David spoke sober truth in that noble and manly lamentation when he said, "Thy love was wonderful to me, passing the love of women."

And it is love that seeks you and me to-day. It is a love that longs to gain our friendship. It is a love that had been told to us, but at last was shown to us in the death of the cross. And we know it is true. David responded to the love that was shown him. He did not disappoint his friend. May the Lord save you and me from disappointing our Friend. "For He is a Friend that sticketh closer than a brother."

VI

THE WOMAN OF THE SHATTERED ROMANCES—THE WOMAN OF SYCHAR

John 4: 4-26

Look, will you, at this picture. There sits a man in the strength and buoyancy of young manhood. He is only thirty or thereabouts. About him is the atmosphere of vigor and vitality that belong to the springtime of life. But to-day he is a bit tired. There is a droop in his shoulders. His feet and sandals are dusty. His garment is travel stained. He has been journeying all the morning on foot. And now at the noon hour he is resting.

The place of his resting is an old well curb. The well is one that was digged by hands that have been dust long centuries. This traveller is very thirsty. But he has no means of drawing the water, so he sits upon the well curb and waits. His friends who are journeying with him have gone into the city to buy food. Soon they will return and then they will eat and drink together.

As he looks along the road that leads into the city he sees somebody coming. That somebody is not one of his disciples. It is a woman. As she comes closer he sees that she is clad in the cheap and soiled finery of her class. At once he knows her for what she is. He reads the dark story of her sinful life. He understands the whole fetid and filthy past through which she has journeyed as through the stenchful mud of a swamp.

As she approaches the well she glares at the Stranger seated upon the curb with bold and unsympathetic gaze. She knows his nationality at once. And all her racial resentment is alive and active.

A bit to her surprise the Stranger greets her with a request for a favor. "Give me a drink," he says. Christ was thirsty. He wanted a draught from Jacob's well. But far more He wanted a draught from this woman's heart. She was a slattern, an outcast. She was lower, in the estimation of the average Jew, than a street dog. Yet this weary Christ desired the gift of her burnt out and impoverished affections. So He says, "Give me to drink."

There is no scorn in the tone, and yet the woman is not in the least softened by it. She rather glories in the fact that she has Him at a disadvantage. "Oh, yes," she doubtless says to herself, "you Jews with your high-handed pride, you Jews with your bitter contempt for us Samaritans—you never have any use for us except when you need us." "How is it," she says, "that you being a Jew ask drink of me who am a woman of Samaria? You don't mean that you would take a drink at the hand of an unclean thing like me, do you?"

But this charming Stranger does not answer her as she had expected. He makes no apology for His request. Nor does He show the least bit of resentment or contempt. He does not answer scorn with scorn, but rather answers with a surprising tenderness: "If thou knewest the gift of God and who it is that saith unto thee, Give me to drink, thou wouldest have asked of Him and He would have given thee living water."

Mark what the Master says. It is one of those abidingly tragic "ifs"—"If thou knewest." "The trouble with you," He says, "is that you do not know the marvelous opportunity with which you now stand face to face. Your trouble is that you are unaware of how near you are to the Fountain of Eternal Life. You do not realize how near your soiled fingers are to clasping wealth that is wealth forever more."

"If thou knewest"—if you only knew how He could still the fitful fever of your heart. If you only knew the message of courage and hope and salvation that He could speak through your lips, you would not be so listless and so careless and so indifferent as the preacher is trying to preach. If you knew the burdens that are ahead of you—if you knew the dark and lonely places where you will sorely need a friend, you would not lightly ignore the friendship and abiding companionship that is offered you in Christ Jesus, our Lord.

"If thou knewest." Do you not hear the cadences of tenderness in the voice of our Lord? Do you not get a glimpse of some bit of the infinite compassion that looks out from those eternal eyes? "If you only knew the gift of God, if you only knew who I am, instead of my having to beg you, instead of my having to stand at the door and knock—you would be knocking. You would be asking of me."

Now, isn't that a rather amazing thing for Christ to say about this fallen woman? There she stands in her shame. Once, no doubt, she was beautiful. There is a charm about her still in spite of the fact that she is a woman of many a shattered romance. Five times she has been married, but the marriage relationship has had little sacredness for her. Her orange blossoms have been dipped in pitch and to-day she is living in open sin.

Who would ever have expected any marked change in this woman? Who would ever have dreamed that

underneath this cheap and tarnished dress there beat
a hungry heart? Who would ever have thought that
this outcast heathen had moments when she looked wist-
fully toward the heights and longed for a better life?
I suppose nobody would ever have thought of it but
the kindly Stranger who now sat upon the well curb
talking to her. He knew that in spite of her wasted
years, in spite of her tarnished past, in spite of the
fact that the foul breath of passion had blown her
about the streets as a filthy rag—there still was that
within her that hungered and thirsted for goodness and
for God.

And, my friend, you may assume that that thirst
belongs to every man. There is not one that is not
stirred by it. It belongs to the best of mankind.
It belongs to the elect company of white souled men
and women that have climbed far up the hills toward
God. It belongs to the great saints like David who
cries, "My soul thirsteth for God, for the living God,"
who sobs out in his intensity of longing, "As the hart
panteth after the water brook, so panteth my soul after
thee, O God."

And thank God it does not belong to the saints alone.
It belongs also to the sinners. It does not belong simply to those who have climbed toward the heights, but
also to those who have dipped toward the lowest depths.
About the only difference between the saint and the
sinner in this respect is that the saint knows what
he is thirsting for. He knows who it is that can satisfy
the deepest longings of his soul, and the sinner does
not know. But both of them are thirsting for the
living God.

Jesus Christ knew men and women. He knew the
human heart, and knowing man at his deepest, He

knew what we sometimes forget. He knew that in every man, however low, however degraded he may be—that in every woman, however soiled and stained she may be, there is an insatiable longing for God. They do not always realize that for which they are thirsting. But I am absolutely sure that Augustine was right when he said that "God has made us for Himself and we never find rest till we rest in Him." Every human soul that is in the Far Country is in want, is hungry for the Bread of Life and thirsty for the Water of Life.

Do you remember what the Greeks said to Andrew that day at Jerusalem? "'Sir, we would see Jesus.' We would have a vision of the face of God's Son." And this is a universal longing. It is a thirst that has burned in the heart of man from the beginning of human history. It is older than the pyramids. It is a cry that is the very mother of religion.

As we sit by our Lord and see this unclean woman coming with her earthenware pot upon her shoulder we would fain warn Him. We would whisper in His ear, "Look, Master, yonder comes a degraded woman, yonder comes that creature that in all the centuries has been the most loathed and the most despised and who has been regarded as the most hopeless. Yonder comes an outcast." But Jesus said, "You see and know only in part. Your knowledge is surface knowledge. You do not know her in the deepest depths of her soiled soul. Yonder comes one, who in spite of her sin longs to be good and pure and holy. Yonder comes an immortal soul with immortal hungers and thirsts. Yonder comes a possible child of mine that longs ignorantly but passionately for the under-girding of the Everlasting Arms."

And believe me, my friends, when I tell you that this longing is universal. You have feared to speak to that acquaintance of yours who seems so flippant, who seems so utterly indifferent to everything that partakes of the nature of religion. But that is not the deepest fact about him. Whoever he is and wherever he is, there are times when he is restless and heartsick and homesick. There are times when he is literally parched with thirst for those fountains that make glad the city of God. Dare to speak to him as if he wanted Jesus Christ. For he does want Him, though he may not know it and may be little conscious of it.

"If thou knewest the gift of God . . . thou wouldest have asked of Him." That was absolutely and literally true, though I seriously doubt if the woman herself would have believed it of herself. If you knew the gift of God, if you knew what God could do for you, how much he could mean to your wasted and burnt out affections—you would ask Him. You would seek for Him. You would change this well curb into an altar of prayer. You would change this noon-tide glare into an inner temple, into a holy of holies where the soul and God would meet and understand each other.

This reply of the Stranger awakens the interest of the woman while at the same time it mystifies and bewilders her. He is evidently sincere, and yet what can He mean? And in puzzled wonderment she asks. Him, "Whence then hast thou living water? You have nothing to draw with and the well is deep. Are you greater than our father Jacob who gave us the well and drank thereof himself and his sons and his cattle? Jacob was a great prince, a man of power with God and man. Do you know a secret that he did not know? Can you do what he could not do?"

And this winsome Stranger does not hesitate to say that He can. Will you listen to the claim that He makes to this woman. No other teacher however great and however egotistical ever made such a claim before or since. "Yes," He replies, "I am greater than your father Jacob. I am greater because I can give a gift that is infinitely beyond his. 'Every one that drinketh of this water shall thirst again, but whosoever drinketh of the water that I shall give him shall never thirst. But the water that I shall give him shall be in him a well of water springing up into everlasting life.'"

Did you notice here the two-fold declaration of the Master? He said in the first place that this old well would not satisfy permanently. And what is true of that well is true of all wells that have ever been digged by human hands. What is wrong with them? For one thing, they never satisfy. They never slake our thirst. To drink from them is like drinking sea water—we become only the more parched and thirsty as we drink.

Do you remember "The Ancient Mariner"? He is on a ship in the ocean and he is parched and dying with thirst. What is the matter? Has the sea gone dry? No—

> "Water, water everywhere
> And all the boards did shrink;
> Water, water everywhere,
> Nor any drop to drink."

There is water, but it is not water that will satisfy.

And so men have digged their wells. They have been real wells. They had held real water of a kind, but it has been water that was utterly powerless to slake the thirst of the soul. Here is a man who has digged a well of wealth. Treasure is bubbling up about him like the waters of a fountain. He is rich beyond his hopes, but is he satisfied? Listen! "Soul, thou hast much good laid up for many days, eat, drink and be merry." But his soul has no appetite for that kind of bread. His soul has no thirst for that brackish and bitter water. It is hungry and thirsty for the living God, and nothing else can satisfy.

Here is another who has made the same tragic blunder.

"I'm an alien—I'm an alien to the faith my mother taught me;
   I'm an alien to the God that heard my mother when she cried;
I'm a stranger to the comfort that my 'Now I lay me' brought me,
   To the Everlasting Arms that held my father when he died.
I have spent a life-time seeking things I spurned when I had found them;
   I have fought and been rewarded in full many a winning cause;
But I'd yield them all—fame, fortune and the pleasures that surround them;
   For a little of the faith that made my mother what she was.

"When the great world came and called me I deserted all to follow,
   Never knowing, in my dazedness, I had slipped my hand from His—
Never noting, in my blindness, that the bauble fame was hollow,
   That the gold of wealth was tinsel, as I since have learned it is—
I have spent a life-time seeking things I've spurned when I have found them;
   I have fought and been rewarded in full many a petty cause,
But I'd take them all—fame, fortune and the pleasures that surround them,
   And exchange them for the faith that made my mother what she was."

Here is one who has dug a well of fame, but he cannot count up twelve happy days. And though he has drunk draughts that might have quenched the thirst of millions, he is dying of thirst because there is no more to drink.

> "Oh, could I feel as once I felt,
>   And be what I have been,
>   And weep as I could once have wept
>   O'er many a vanished scene.
>
> "As springs in deserts found seem sweet,
>   All brackish though they be;
>   So midst the withered waste of life
>   Those tears would flow to me."

"Oh, what is fame to a woman," said another. "Like the apples of the Dead Sea, fair to the sight and ashes to the touch." Here is another and he has digged wells of wealth and fame and power and pleasure. He seems afloat upon a very sea in which all the streams of human power and glory and wisdom mingle. He tastes them all only to dash the cup from his lips in loathing and disgust as he cries, "Vanity of vanities! All is vanity and vexation of spirit."

And so Jesus says to this woman, "This well can never permanently satisfy you. No well of this world can. But if you are only willing, I can give you a well that will satisfy. I can impart that which will meet every single need and every single longing of your soul." What a claim is this! How marvelous, how amazing! And yet this tired young man, sitting here by the well, makes this high claim, and through the centuries He has made it good.

"I can give you," says He, "a well that will satisfy you now. I can touch the hot fever of your life into restfulness now. I can satisfy the intensest hunger of your starved soul even now. And not only can I do this for the present, but I can satisfy for all eternity. I can give you a fountain that will never run dry. I can bless your life with a springtime where the trees will never shed their leaves and the petals of the rose will never shatter upon the grass."

"If you will allow me, I will give you that which will enrich and satisfy your life to-day and to-morrow and through all the eternal to-morrow." In all world feasts there comes a time when we have to say, "There is no wine." There comes a time when the zest is gone, when the wreaths are withered. There comes a time when joy lies coffined and we have left to us only the dust and ashes of burnt out hopes. But Christ satisfies now and ever more. And this He does in spite of all circumstances and in the presence of all difficulties. For His is not an external fountain to which we have to journey again and again and from which we may be cut off by the forces of the enemy. His is a fountain within. It is that which makes us independent of our foes and even, when need be, of our friends. Dr. Jowett tells how he visited an old, ruined castle in England and found far in the inner precincts of that castle a gurgling and living spring.

What a treasure it was to the man who lived in that castle! His enemies might besiege him and shut him in, but they could never cut off his water supply. No foes however great were able to overcome him by starvation for water because he had a fountain within. There was within the castle a well of water springing up, and he was independent of all outside sources.

Now, when Jesus had told this woman of the wonderful gift that He had the power of imparting it is not at all strange that she answered, "Sir, give me this water that I thirst not, neither come all the way here to draw." And that is just what Jesus desires above all else to do for her. But there is one something in the way. Before Christ can impart His saving and satisfying gift the woman must be brought face to face with her need. She must be made to face her own sin eye to eye and to hate it and confess it. She must be willing to turn from it to Him who is able to cleanse from all sin by the washing of His blood.

And how tactfully does Christ bring her face to face with her past! Nothing could be more tenderly delicate than His touch here. "Go call thy husband," He says. "I have no husband," is the ready response. And then He compliments her.

If you are to be successful as a soul winner, if you are to be successful as a worker anywhere—it is fine to have an eye for that which is praiseworthy. There is something commendable about everybody if we only seek for it and find it. A disreputable dog came to our house the other day. My wife looked at him and said, "What a horrible looking dog!" But our small boy looked at him with a different eye and found something good about him and remarked that he could wag his tail well.

There was not much in this woman to compliment. But Jesus picked out one thing that was commendable. He complimented her on the fact that she had told Him the truth. He said, "You have been honest in this. You have no husband. You have had five husbands, but the man that thou now hast is not thy husband. In that saidst thou truly." And now the woman stands looking her soiled and stained past eye to eye.

She does not like it. She would like to get away from it. She wants to start a theological discussion. She is ready to launch out into an argument over the proper place to worship God. But Christ holds her face to face with her sin till she loathes it, and utters that deepest cry of her inner nature, the longing for the coming of the Messiah. And then it is that Christ made the first disclosure of Himself that He ever made in this world. He seems to lift the veil from the face of the infinite as He says, "I that speak unto thee am He."

And this woman has found the Living Water. She forgot her old thirst. She forgot the errand that brought her to the well. She left the empty water pot by the curbstone and bounded away like a happy child into the city. She is under the compelling power of a marvelous discovery. She has a story infinitely too good to keep. And in spite of the fact that her past had been a shameful and sordid past—she would not let it close her lips. She gave her testimony, and as a result we read these words, "Many believed because of the saying of the woman."

Heart, this woman never had your chance and mine. She was placed in a bad setting. She wasted the best years of her life. She never found Jesus till the sweetest and freshest years of her life had been squandered in sin. She only met him in the last lingering days of autumn or maybe in the winter time of life. Though she met Him so late, when she stood in His presence a little later in glory she had her hands full of sheaves.

You have had a great chance. Is there anybody that believes because of what you have said? Has any life been transfigured and transformed by the story that you have told? Will you not give a little more earnestness and a little more thought and a little more prayer and a little more effort to the doing of this work that Jesus Christ did not think was beneath Himself as the King of Heaven and the Savior of the world?

And if you have never found the fountain that satisfies, if you know nothing of the spring that flows within —will you not claim that blessed treasure now? Will you not do so, first of all, because of your own needs? Then will you not do so not only because of your own needs but because of the needs of those about you? You are thirsty men and women, and this is a thirsty world. You need God and God needs you. Will you give Him a chance at you?

Remember that this well of water is not to be yours on the basis of merit. It is not to be bought. It is not to be earned. It is not found in the pathway of the scholar or of the rich or of the great or of the gifted. It is God's gift. If you want wages serve the devil, for "the wages of sin is death." "But the gift of God is eternal life through Jesus Christ, our Lord."

In oriental cities, where water is often scarce, water carriers go through the streets selling water at so much per drink. And their cry is this: "The gift of God, who will buy? Who will buy?" And sometimes a man will buy the whole supply, and then allow the water carrier to give it away. And as he goes back down the street, he no longer says, "The gift of God, who will buy?" but "The gift of God, who will take? The gift of God, who will take?" That is my message to you: "The gift of God, who will take?" It is yours for the taking. May God help you to take it now.

VII

A GOOD MAN—BARNABAS

Acts 11:24

This is the text: "He was a good man." Doubtless
you think me daring to the point of rashness to undertake to interest and edify a modern congregation by
talking about a virtue so prosaic as goodness. "He
was a good man." We do not thrill when we hear
that. It is not a word that quickens our pulse beat.
We do not sit up and lean forward. We rather relax
and stifle a yawn and look at our watches and wonder
how soon it will be over. We are interested in clever
men, in men of genius. We are interested in bad men,
in courageous men, in poor men and rich men, but
good men—our interest lags here, nods, drowses, goes
to sleep.

The truth of the matter is that the word "good"
is a bit like the poor fellow that went down from
Jerusalem to Jericho. It has fallen among thieves that
have stripped it of its raiment and have wounded it and
departed, leaving it half dead. It is a word that has
a hospital odor about it. It savors of plasters and
poultices and invalid chairs. Its right hand has no
cunning. Its tongue has no fire. Its cheeks are corpse-
like in their paleness. It seems to be in the last stages
of consumption. If people say we are handsome or
cultured we are delighted, but who is complimented by
being called good?

What has wrecked this word? What is the secret

of its weakness and utter insipidity? Answer: bad company. The Book says, "The companion of fools shall be destroyed." And this word is an example of the truth of that statement. It has been forced to rub elbows with bad company till it has come into utter disrepute.

Its evil companions have been of two classes. First, it has been made to associate with the gentleman about town whose greatest merit was that he would smoke a cigar with you, if you would furnish the cigar, or take a drink with you, if you would furnish the liquor. He also graced a dress suit, even though it were a rented one with the rent unpaid. And he looked well in pumps. He was a graceful dancer and good at poker. He also was very skilled in never having a job. And his friends all said that "he was a good fellow." And, of course, being forced to keep company with said fellow was enough to ruin the reputation of the word forever more.

But as if that were not enough calamity to befall any innocent and inoffensive word, it was forced into another association that was but little less disreputable. There was an individual—sometimes a man, sometimes a woman—who did not swear, nor lie, nor steal, nor dip snuff; whose conduct was as immaculate as that of a wax figure in a show window; who never made a mistake, nor did he ever make anything else. He was as aggressive as a crawfish and as magnetic as a mummy. He was "faultily faultless, icily regular, splendidly null." And one day we felt called upon to clothe this colorless insipidity, this incarnate nonentity, with some sort of an adjective, and so we threw around its scrawny shoulders this once glorious robe "good." We said, "Yes, he isn't much account, it is true, but he is a good fellow." And the garment fit him as the coat of Goliath would fit a pigmy. But little by little the once great cloak seemed to draw up and to come to fit the figure of the dwarf.

Thus the word "good" lost its reputation, fell, as many words and many folks do fall, through bad company. But let me remind you that, in spite of popular misconception, "good" is not after all a weak word. It is a strong, brawny, masculine word. It has the shoulders of a Samson. It has the lifting power of a Hercules. And the reason God employed it here to describe this man Barnabas was not because He had to say something about him and could not find anything else decent to say. It was not a word to cover up the deformity of uselessness or the glaring defect of a moral minus sign. He used the word because there was none other that would fitly describe the fine and heroic man of whom He was speaking. It means here all that "Christian" means.

"He was a good man." That was what God said about him. That was how he looked when seen through "the microscope of Calvary." He had matriculated in God's school, and after faithful and patient study, his Master gave him a degree. And what was that degree? Barnabas, the genius? No. Barnabas, the gifted? No. It was a higher degree than either of these. It was the highest degree that Heaven itself can confer. He gave him the degree of "good." Barnabas, the good. "For he was a good man."

Now, why did God call him good? Or, in other words, what are the characteristics that go to make up a good man? When is a man good in the sight of "Him who sees things clearly and sees them whole?" In what branches must a man show himself proficient in order to receive this degree? I ask these questions with the hope that some of us who are here to-day may want to matriculate in God's school to receive the high degree that was conferred upon Barnabas.

The first branch in which Barnabas showed himself proficient in his preparation for this degree was the branch of Christian Stewardship. And I make bold to say that no man will ever receive the degree that Barnabas received who is not proficient in the grace of stewardship.

Here is the story. Barnabas is in Jerusalem at the time of Pentecost. The Church is in the early spring-time of its power. Many Jews, both home-born and foreign-born, have been brought into the fold. They have thereby broken with their kindred, and many of them are without any means of support. Then Barnabas comes forward. He is a wealthy land owner. He sells his land and puts every dollar of it upon the altar of his Lord, for the saving of the church in its hour of crisis.

What does this mean? It means that when Barnabas became a Christian, that when he gave himself to Christ, he gave his money also. Now, stewardship for you may not mean that you, as Barnabas, sell what you have and give it all away. God does not call upon all men to do that, but what He does do is to call upon every man to put both himself and his money at His disposal. He calls upon every man to recognize God, and not himself, as the owner. That is the first step in Christian Stewardship: that God owns all; He owns me; He owns my home; He owns my children; He owns my property. I have called your attention before to the fact that the modern idea of ownership is pagan.

The Christian idea is this: that God is the absolute owner of all things.

I am sure that we are as ready as was Barnabas to acknowledge this fact. We nod our heads and agree, but a truth like this demands something more than simply a nod of the head. If God owns everything, then I am to acknowledge that ownership. How was God's ownership acknowledged throughout all the Old Testament days? By the devoting of a tenth to His service. That was required of the rich and of the poor. No man was exempt. Christ never at any time set that law aside. I do not see how any man dare do less than that to-day. The Jews, without one thousandth part of our light, were cursed because of their failure to do this very thing. Since when has it come to pass that the greater the light the less the responsibility?

There is nothing more needed to-day than a Christian attitude toward money. There has been a reaction from the altruism that prevailed during the war, and the world is more money mad than ever before. And men are making money as scarcely ever before, and the man who is making money is the man who stands in the position of a peculiar danger. For the men who can rapidly accumulate money and at the same time be loyal to Jesus Christ are few indeed.

While I was in Dallas the other day I talked to a friend who was a man of wealth. He said without enthusiasm, "I have made more money this year than I ever made before." And then I questioned him regarding his work in the Church. At one time he had been the teacher of a very large class of boys. He told me that he had given up his Sunday School work, that he had given up all his religious work. Then I said, "If you had a thermometer for registering happiness, I suppose your thermometer would register lower to-day than at any other time since you came into the Church." And with sadness he acknowledged that such was the case.

Yes, Barnabas was sound in the doctrine of stewardship. And I am fully persuaded that the man who is genuinely Christian in his attitude toward money will be Christian in every other relationship of life. And I am likewise fully persuaded that the man who fails here, who falls short of the standard of goodness here, will fall short everywhere. A man may be a liberal man and fail to be a good man, but no man can be a good man and at the same time be a gripping, grasping, covetous man. It is an utter impossibility. Barnabas got a degree in goodness, and the first course he mastered was a course in Christian Stewardship.

Second, Barnabas was proficient in that difficult branch that we call faith. He had acquired faith till he was full of it. Faith in God? Yes, he had faith in God. That lies back of all that he did and all that he became. But the faith that shows itself most in his life, as we see it, is his faith in men. How he did believe in folks! Confidence in men is an essential to true goodness. I do not believe that any cynic was ever a really good man. I know we sometimes pride ourselves on being hard to fool. We congratulate ourselves at times on being able to see more through a keyhole than other folks can see through a wide-open door. We boast of our ability to read character and to see behind the scenes and to detect sham where other folks dreamed there was sincerity. And I am not arguing for blindness or stupidity, but what I do say is this: that the really good men are the men who believe in their fellows.

You have met the man who says that every fellow has his price. But whenever you hear a man say that you may know that there is at least one man who does have his price, and that is the man who is making the statement. You can compromise till you come to persuade yourself that compromise is the law of life. You can play with honesty till you come to believe in the dishonesty of the whole world. And the man without confidence in his brother is a man who personally knows that he himself would not do to trust.

Barnabas believed in men. One of the greatest enemies that the Church ever had returned one day from a tour of persecution in Damascus. He declared that he had been converted on the way, but nobody in Jerusalem believed him. Yes, there was one glorious exception. That exception was Barnabas. He believed in Paul, staked his reputation, his life, his Church, which was dearer to him than his life,—he staked all these upon his faith in Paul's sincerity. But for that, Paul might have been lost to the Church.

And here is another instance: Paul and Barnabas are on their first missionary tour. With them is a young man named Mark. He has been tenderly nurtured. He finds the missionary life harder than he expected. He proves a coward and goes home. Years after, when the faces of Paul and Barnabas are again set to the battle front, Mark once more offers his service. But Paul will not accept him. He knows that the mission field is no place for parlor soldiers. And so he flatly refuses to allow him to become a part of the army of invasion.

But Barnabas,—somehow he cannot bring himself to give him up. He believes that even if a man failed once he may succeed at a second trial. He believes that a coward may become a hero, that a deserter may yet become a trusted and faithful soldier. And so he stands by John Mark even at the great price of parting company with Paul. And his confidence was gloriously justified, as our confidence so often is. Who wrote the second Gospel—one of the choicest pieces of literature in the world? It was written by John Mark, the deserter.

Then years later, when bitter days of persecution have come, Paul is in prison. He especially needs men about him now on whose loyal courage and devotion he can count absolutely. For whom does he now ask? Listen! "Take Mark and bring him with thee, for he is profitable to me for the ministry." Mark has come back. He has been saved to Christ and to the Church. And the one to whom we are mainly indebted for his salvation is none other than the good man Barnabas. And Barnabas won because of his sturdy, persistent faith.

Now to some this virtue may seem a bit of a weakness, but if weakness, how like it is to the weakness of Christ Himself! For certainly one of the most marvelous characteristics of Jesus is His faith in men. How Jesus could expect that the poor slattern who was dragged into His presence taken in adultery could be utterly different from that hour, I do not know. I certainly would not have expected it of her, but He did. And I hear Him saying to her, "Go and sin no more." How Jesus could expect that twelve faulty, unlearned, self-seeking men, such as His disciples were, would ever be the means of remaking the world, I cannot for a moment see. They failed Him in His hour of supremest need. They slept in the garden and ran like frightened sheep when He was arrested. And yet, knowing their cowardice and their weakness, He tumbles the responsibility of world conquest upon their frail shoulders with the declaration that "the gates of hell should not prevail against them." Certainly the wildest faith that was ever exercised is the faith that God exercises in men. And the faith of this man Barnabas was a quality born of a goodness that was close akin to the goodness of God.

That is the way, I think, that this man got his name. You know they did not always call him Barnabas. The folks over in Cypress knew him as Joses. They named him Barnabas because that was the word that best described him. It was a verbal picture of the man. What does it mean? A son of consolation. Isn't that fine? James and John were called the sons of thunder. That speaks of power, might, dash, the lightning's flash, the thunder's crash. There is storm wrapped up in their personalities. But Barnabas is the peaceful sunset after the storm. He is the light at eventide. He is a son of consolation.

Now, if there is anything finer than that I do not know just what that something might be. To be incarnated encouragement, embodied comfort, flesh and blood consolation,—it would be hard to find a better vocation than that. This man had the tongue of the learned that he might be able to speak a word in season to him that was weary. He delivered men from the bondage of their self-despisings, from the burden of their self-contempt. He brought hope where there had been despair and turned the westward gaze toward the east. He pointed out the streaks of dawn that were lighting the sky. He made men hear the bird's song within the voiceless egg and to catch the perfume of flowers under the snow. He was a son of consolation. "Be pitiful," says Dr. Watson, "for every man is having a hard time." There are some folks who depress us. There are some wet blanket personalities who stifle us. And there are others like Barnabas who refresh us, and when they come and knock at our doors we pass out of the stuffy atmosphere of a mental prison into a flower garden where the air is fresh and sweet with perfume and musical with the morning song of birds.

Third, this man was thoroughly missionary. He had taken a course in God's doctrine of evangelism. He believed that the Gospel was for all mankind. Some Christians of that day were trying to keep it a Jewish sect. When they heard that folks were actually being converted down in Antioch there seems to have been not the least bit of joy in the fact. But under the leadership of the Spirit they sent Barnabas to investigate. He came and saw the same light in their faces down in Antioch that was in the faces of those who were Spirit-baptized up in Jerusalem. And the story says that when he saw the work of the Lord he was glad. And not only was he glad, but he threw himself at once into the work of evangelizing that foreign city.

Then he did another big thing. Seeing the great opportunity that was there, he went and sought Paul out over at Tarsus and brought him over as his helper. And it was there as they labored together and ministered to the Lord and fasted that the Holy Ghost said, "Separate me Barnabas and Saul, for the work whereunto I have called them." And they went forth as the world's first foreign missionaries. An army has gone forth since that day,—the choicest spirits that this world has ever seen. And those who have gone have consecrated the soil of every continent by their prayers, their tears and their sacrifices. Their ashes rest to-day upon every shore and the songs of the redeemed are sung to-day under every sky because they have labored. Who was the vanguard of that great army whose going forth was as the going forth of the morning? The vanguard was made up of two men. One of them was Paul, the other Barnabas, a man not marvelously clever, not greatly gifted. His supreme merit was just this, that in a real and genuine sense he was a good man, full of faith.

And last of all, Barnabas was a spiritual man. The inspired writer says that he was full of the Holy Ghost. And that implied, of course, that Barnabas was a man fully given up to God. There can be no deep spirituality apart from that. Our surrender is the condition of our being full of the Spirit. "For we are His witnesses of these things, as is also the Holy Ghost, whom God hath given to them that obey Him."

So you can readily see why Barnabas has a right to the fine compliment that is paid him here by the writer of the Acts. Barnabas was generous with his possessions. He had the Christian attitude toward money. Barnabas was generous in his judgments. He had a brother's attitude toward his fellows. He was thoroughly missionary. He made Christ's program for world conquest his own. He was profoundly and genuinely spiritual. And because of these fine qualities one who knew him well said of him, "He was a good man."

Now, there are compliments more flashy than being called good. There are encomiums that are much fuller of glitter, but in spite of that, I am convinced that nothing greater or better could possibly be said about any

one of us living to-day or any one that ever has lived
than just this that is written about Barnabas: "He
was a good man." I had rather my boy would be able
to say that about me when he stands by my grave,
sunken and grass-grown, than to say anything else in all
the world.

Brother, let us covet goodness. Let us seek that
rare treasure. For there is nothing better or finer
or more beautiful or more useful. "Goodness."
It is the fairest flower that can ever bloom in your
soul garden. It is the sweetest music that even God's
skilled fingers will ever be able to win from your thousand stringed heart harp. It is the virtue in those
we love that grips us tightest and holds us longest.
And wonderful to say, it is within reach of every one
of us.

There are certain fine things that you and I
can never possess. We know that. Genius, greatness,
—they are high and forbidding mountain peaks. Their
sides are rugged and precipitous. They have pulled
iron hoods of snow and ice upon their brows. But
goodness,—that is a peak that may be scaled by the tender feet of little children and by the tottering feet of
old age. It may be scaled by the reluctant feet of those
in life's prosaic middle passage. Let us address ourselves then to this high task. Let us matriculate this
morning in God's school for this degree, the degree of
"goodness." And one day it may be written of us as
it was written of Barnabas, "He was a good man."

VIII

THE INQUEST—PHARAOH

Exodus 14:30 *and* 9:16

In Exodus 14:19 we read these words: "And Israel saw the Egyptians dead upon the seashore." It is rather a ghastly and grewsome sight. There they lie, the soldiers of the once proud army of Egypt. They are in all sorts of positions, these dead men. Some have their heads pillowed peacefully upon their arms as if in sleep. Others have their hard faces half buried in the sand. Others still lie prone upon their backs with bits of seaweed in their hair and their sightless eyes staring in terror at nothing.

They are very much alike, these corpses. But here is one that is different. Look at the rich costume in which it is dressed. Look at its bejewelled fingers. There is no crown upon its brow. There is no sceptre in that nerveless hand. Yet it is easy to guess that this corpse, this "pocket that death has turned inside out and emptied" was once a king. Yes, this is the body of Pharaoh, the one time ruler of Egypt. But here he lies to-day among the meanest of his soldiers. He is sprawled in unkingly fashion upon his face as if the sea had spit him out in sheer nausea and disgust.

And now comes the big question that we want to consider. How came this famous Egyptian here? He was once a king, you remember. He was ruler over the proudest nation in the world. And here we find

him dead. He died away from home. He died a
violent death. Let us hold an inquest over him for
a moment and see how he came to die. He did not
leave Egypt and march into the Red Sea for that purpose. He never intended that life should end thus.
Nor is he here because his enemy Israel has proven
stronger than himself. What is the cause? And the
question is answered by the voice of God. We read
it in Exodus 9:16, "For this cause have I raised thee
up that I might show forth my power in thee."

Will you notice what this strange text says. Without
the least equivocation it says that God raised this man
Pharaoh up that He might show forth His power in
him. And that purpose He accomplished. This ghastly
piece of royal rottenness has not been thrown upon
this shore by the hand of man. As we look at him
we see in him a monument of the power of God. And
strange to say, he is not a monument of God's power
to save and to keep and to utilize, but of God's power
to thwart and to disappoint and to wreck and to utterly
destroy. And in his destruction God tells us that He
has achieved His purpose.

You will agree with me that this is an amazing statement. The teaching seems to be that God has raised this
man up that He might glorify Himself by making a
complete and utter wreck of him. I wonder if that can
be true. We agree, I suppose, all of us who believe the
Bible, that God has a plan for every life. All nature
tells of a planning God. All revelation teaches it also.
We have the message direct from the lips of the Lord,
"As my Father hath sent me, even so send I you."

But in admitting that God plans every life, can
we believe that He plans for some to go wrong and
for others to go right? Can we believe that He plans

for one to become a Judas and the other a St. John?
Is it the purpose of God that one shall develop into
a Moses and the other right at his side shall grow
up into a miserable and distorted wreck that we call
Pharaoh? In other words, is Judas as much a part of
the plan of God as John? If so we are of all men
most miserable because we have a wicked God.

But we know that such is not the case. God never
planned that any man should go wrong. He is not
willing that any should perish, but that all should come
to repentance. He is the eternal lover. He loved
Moses, but He loved Pharaoh no less. And
Judas was as dear to God's heart as John. And whatever failure they made of their lives, and whatever
failure you and I make of our lives, we do not make
because God forces us to do so. In whatever way we
go wrong, we do not do so because God planned that
we should. We do it because of our own willfulness and
wicked rebellion against God.

In other words, though God plans your life and
mine, He cannot in the very nature of things, force
us to enter into His plan. You who are fathers and
mothers realize that. Many parents have made beautiful plans for their children only to have those plans
despised. Our children are not ourselves. They have
independent wills. They have the capacity for entering
into our purposes for them and thus bringing us joy
unspeakable. They have also the capacity for despising
those purposes and breaking our hearts.

How, then, do we explain this strange text, "For
this cause have I raised thee up that I might show forth
my power in thee"? Because it is a fact that this
death in the Red Sea was not an accidental death. It
is a fact that this corpse here upon the beach is not

here by mere chance. This king was flung here by the power of a disappointed and grieved and rejected God. He lies here dead upon the shore according to the deliberate plan and purpose of God. But while this is true, we need to keep this big fact in mind: Though Pharaoh lies here according to the purpose of God, this was not God's first and highest purpose for him. But Pharaoh resisted and rejected every noble and worthy purpose that God had in his life. By his own rebellion he made it impossible for God to realize any purpose in him at all save the last and the worst.

Do you remember that story in Jeremiah? One day the word of the Lord came unto the prophet Jeremiah saying, "Arise and go down to the Potter's house and there I will cause thee to hear my word." And Jeremiah went down and heard the message. Arrived within the Potter's house, three objects at once drew his attention. There was a man working, the Potter. There was the instrument with which he worked, the wheel. And there was the substance upon which he worked, the clay. In the Potter's hand the clay was misshapen and unsightly. The cup was not yet finished in the Potter's hand. But there was a place where it was finished, and that was in the mind of the Potter. The Potter could already see the finished product. He was trying to make the cup according to the ideal that he had in his mind.

But we read that the cup was marred in the making That is, there was something in the clay that resisted the Potter. Now, what did he do with the marred cup? We would have expected him to throw it away, but he did not. He made it again. What a gospel that is for failing and sinning men like ourselves. How glorious that, when we resist God's purpose, and all but wreck ourselves, He will make us again. Truly we would be a hopeless race but for the fact that we have a mighty God who is able to remake us even when we have rebelled against Him and have thwarted His blessed plans for us.

He made it again. Yes, but notice this. He made it again "another vessel." He changed his plan for this latter vessel. He realized that he could not make it according to the fine ideal that was in his mind for the first vessel. That one refused to realize the best, therefore he made it into another vessel. He sought to make it realize the second best.

There is a truth here of tremendous importance that we are prone to forget, and that truth is this, that having rejected and resisted God for days and months and years, God cannot make of us what He could have made if we had entered into His plans from the beginning. If you reject God's best for you, then He tries to get you to realize His second best. If you reject this, then He seeks to bring you to the next best. But remember this, God cannot, in the very nature of things, make as much out of a fraction of a life as He can out of the whole of a life.

Now, suppose, the clay upon which the Potter was working had been marred again. Again he would have undertaken to have made it into another vessel. But all the while that clay would have been becoming less and less plastic. All the while it would have been becoming more and more difficult for the Potter to shape it according to his purpose.

Thus the time would inevitably come when it would no longer be capable of being shaped by his hand at all. Then what would be the result? Step outside the Potter's house and you are in the Potter's field.

About you lie broken crockery and shattered earthenware. Why is it there? Not because the Potter made vessels for the stupid purpose of breaking them to pieces. They are there because there was something in the clay that so resisted the hand of the Potter that he was able to make nothing of them but these shattered and misshapen and broken wrecks.

Now this is the story of Pharaoh, king of Egypt. God had a noble purpose in this man's life to begin with. He gave him every opportunity. He brought to bear all that infinite love and mercy could bring to bear to get Pharaoh to be a good man. The reason Pharaoh ended as he did end was not because God did not love him and did not do His infinite best to save Him. It was because Pharaoh resisted and resisted, rebelled and rebelled till at last he threw himself a corpse upon this distant seashore. And the message we hear from his clammy lips this night is this, "Look at me and see what a terrible thing it is to rebel against God. Behold me and see the tragic failure of the man that persistently throws himself in wicked madness against the bosses of the buckler of the Lord Almighty."

Look now how hard God tried to make something of Pharaoh. In the first place, He gave to him a great and faithful minister. Pharaoh had the privilege of knowing Moses. He had an opportunity of hearing about the greatest individual that the world has ever seen. He threw himself away, did Pharaoh. He chose God's worst instead of God's best, but he did not do it because he did not know better. Neither are you wasting your life because you do not know better. If you have not had a teacher great as Moses, you have yet been faithfully warned, and in your sin you are without excuse.

God gave Pharaoh a chance to coöperate with Him, to help Him in saving Israel and making her into a great nation. Moses' first word to Pharaoh was this, "The God of Israel saith, Let my people go." Now, Pharaoh's answer to this demand was haughty enough. He answers, "Who is the God of Israel? I do not know him." And he didn't, though he might have known Him. But God did not throw him away after this one chance. On the contrary, He gave him ample opportunity to know Him.

With this end in view God brought His infinite energies into play. Wonder after wonder He worked in the presence of Pharaoh by the hand of Moses. At first these wonders were imitated by the magicians. These fakes, by their cunning, made it easy, at least for a while, for Pharaoh to resist God. They helped the King to close his royal eyes to the truth. They helped him to start with decision on his course of rebellion.

But the magicians were soon outdone. Moses began to perform wonders that they could not imitate. And they themselves were forced to believe in the presence and might and reality of God. And they who had helped their king to go wrong, turned to him with this acknowledgment on their lips, "It is the finger of God." But it is easier to lead a man astray than it is to lead him back. It is easier for you, by your godless and worldly life, to lead your children to despise Christ and the Church than it is to lead them back after they have gone astray. Pharaoh listened to the magicians when they counseled him to do wrong, but he turned a deaf ear to them when they counseled him to do right.

Then followed that series of plagues upon Egypt that were always preceded and always followed by this demand of God spoken through the lips of Moses, "Let my people go that they may serve me." You see what God was demanding of Pharaoh. It is the same that He demands of you and me, obedience—that is all. He is commanding us to surrender ourselves to Him, to enter into His purpose. And the one thing that God wanted was the one thing that Pharaoh did not want. But he was becoming afraid and so he proposed to compromise.

In his fright he tells Moses that he will obey. He will let the people go. That is, he said, "I will let part of them go. I will let the men go. Leave the children here." Pharaoh knew that just so long as he kept the children in Egypt, just so long would Israel remain in bondage. And the devil knows to-day just so long as our homes remain unchristianized, just so long will the world remain unchristianized. We will never bring, in the Kingdom by simply seeking to save an adult generation. We must give God a chance at the children or the cause of righteousness is going to be defeated. But if we will save the child, we will surely save the world.

Then Pharaoh offered a second compromise. He said, "I will let you and the children go, but you must leave your cattle and your sheep. You must leave all your flocks and your herds." That is, you may go into Canaan if you must, but leave your business in Egypt. And the devil to-day is perfectly willing that you and I be just as pious and prayerful as we want to be on Sunday, provided we forget all about such things on

Monday. He is willing for you to be devoutly religious if you will only confine your religion to the church. But a religion that does not permeate and purify and uplift and sanctify business and business relations is not the religion of Jesus Christ.

And then Pharaoh offered a third compromise. He said, "I will let the people go, but they must not go far." Why was that? For the very human reason that he wanted the privilege of getting them back. He said, for instance, "I will obey God, but I do not want to promise to make my obedience permanent." You have seen plenty of instances of that. Here is a man who has decided to be a Christian, but he won't join the church. He wants to see how he gets along first. Such a man is already making provision for going back. "Take up thy bed," said the Master to the paralyzed man whom He had healed. He ever wants us to make a complete break with the past.

But the plagues grow worse. Pharaoh is becoming more and more frightened. While the scare is on he promises again and again that he will obey the Lord unconditionally. There was a terrible storm, you remember. The hail stones fell like shrapnel and the lightning dropped from the clouds and fairly played along the earth, and terror gripped the King's heart. And he sends for Moses. When Moses comes he tells him, all atremble, "I have sinned this time. I will let the people go." But when the storm ceases and the sun shines out he is quite ashamed of his weakness. He is so ashamed that he forgets altogether the promise that he made when the fear of death was upon him.

This is a side of human nature that is a bit disgusting, yet we dare not shut our eyes to it. There are scores listening to me at this very moment who have acted for all the world as Pharaoh acted. And you have done so with all the light that he had and far more. I do not know of a man that is in greater danger of being ultimately lost than that man who never cares for religion except when he is scared. Because the truth of the matter is that a man of that kind does not care for goodness or for God at all. Not even in his moments of most abject terror does he want to be truly saved. He simply wants to escape the results of his sin. He does not want to pay the penalty for wrong doing. He wants to defeat the ends of justice. He is not interested in being good and pure and true. He is simply interested in keeping out of hell.

How patient God was with Pharaoh. We are amazed at it till we think how infinitely patient He has been with ourselves. By storm, by black night, by adversity after adversity, God is doing His best to fight Pharaoh back from the Red Sea. He is doing all He can to turn him away from committing suicide in body and suicide in soul. But Pharaoh, as some of ourselves, seemed absolutely greedy for damnation. He seemed completely bent on working out his own utter destruction.

After the king had broken one vow after another and lied and lied and lied again, God brought the last dark providence into his life. He made one final effort to save him from his ruin. Pharaoh was called to kneel by the coffin of his first born. And his hard heart seemed softened at last. By the grave of the Crown Prince he made a solemn vow that he would obey God. And he set about putting the vow into execution at once. And the children of Israel were not only allowed to go, but they were hurried out of Egypt.

At last, at last, we say, with what infinite expense

the man is brought to obey. But would you believe it, the grass had not yet grown green upon the grave of his boy till he forgot his vow and turned back to the old life again. Oh, what a grip sin gets on us. Oh, how blind we become if we persistently refuse to follow the light. So Pharaoh brushed his tears out of his eyes, gathered his army and set out after the departing children of Israel.

I see the bustle and hurry of the setting out. I see the look of hate on the king's face as he comes within sight of his one time slaves. He laughs a mirthless laugh as he sees their predicament. They are shut in on either side. The sea is in front and he and his army in the rear. What a sweet revenge he is going to have.

But look. Something has happened. There is a path through the sea. These hunted slaves are marching in. But it doesn't matter. Wherever Israel can go, the Egyptians can go. So he and his army march in behind. They keep the Israelites in sight. Now in the distance they see that the last Israelite has reached dry land.

And then there is a great shriek that is quickly choked. The waters have come together again. The sea waves roar about these struggling soldiers like liquid hate. The King is forgotten. His men are madly trying to save themselves. A jeweled hand flashes in the light for a moment. There is an oath, a cry for help, a gulp, and silence. And the hungry sea has its prey.

Pharaoh, why are you here? And if those dead lips could speak he would say, "I am here because I persistently refused to obey God. He offered me the best and I spurned it and spurned it again till at last He threw me here. He did it because I made it impossible for Him to do anything else." And as I look at this wreck I think how different the story might have ended. This man might have had a part in the making of a great people. He might have been associated with Moses in giving to the world a new nation. He might even now be in the fellowship of Moses among the tall sons of the morning. For the difference between this man and the great man Moses is not in the fact that God purposed evil for the one and good for the other. It is in this, that one was obedient unto the heavenly vision, that one could say, "The grace that was bestowed upon me was not in vain," and the other resisted and kept resisting till he ran by every blockade that God could put in his path and plunged headlong into destruction.

IX

A SON OF SHAME—JEPHTHAH

Judges 11:35

"I have opened my mouth unto the Lord and I cannot go back." I like these big words. There is a ring of sterling strength in them. They have a robust masculinity that grips my heart. They are not the words of a weakling. They have absolutely no savor of softness or moral flabbiness. They are not cheap. They are high priced words. They are words made costly by a plentiful baptism of tragedy. They are words literally soaked in blood and tears.

This man Jephthah has made a vow. And now the hour is upon him in which it is his duty to make the vow good. His vow involves far more than he ever expected. But that fact does not cause him to be untrue. He has given his promise. Pay day has come. His promise involves measureless sacrifice. To keep it is to put out every star in his sky. It is to pluck up every flower in his garden. It is to change life's music into discord. It is to take from him the one he loves far better than he loves his own life. But even though the price is big, he will not refuse to pay it. Even though his promise is hard, he will keep it. "I have opened my mouth unto the Lord and I cannot go back."

Jephthah has had many hard things said about him. He has been wronged since before he was born. I do not think that justice has been done to his

memory. Frankly, I think he is one of the most heroic
souls of Old Testament history. It is true that he
would not fully measure up to all our modern ideals,
but remember this, he lived in the morning of human
history. He lived when the light was dim. And he was
true to the light that he had. He was true with a
rugged fidelity that will cause him to rise up in the
day of judgment and condemn many of us.

Jephthah, I say, has been greatly wronged. He never
had a fair chance. He was wronged in his very birth.
He was the son of a father who was unfaithful to his
marriage vows. Jephthah was a child of shame. His
father had chosen to sacrifice upon the wayside altar.
His father had had his fling. He had sown his wild
oats, and of necessity there was a harvest. His father
suffered, but sad to say, he was not the only sufferer.

How we need to be reminded again and again that
no man ever sins alone. No man ever walks from the
path of virtue without he walks upon bruised and bleeding feet. He himself suffers, but what is sadder still, he
causes somebody else to suffer. I cannot go to hell
alone. I cannot plunge out into the dark without
involving another soul, at least in some measure, in
my tragedy. This father sinned. It meant suffering
for him. It also meant suffering for one who was
altogether blameless. It meant suffering for his boy.

Not only did Jephthah have as part of his life tragedy
an unclean father, but he had an unclean mother as
well. Jephthah's mother was not one of those unfortunate souls, more sinned against than sinning, who had
made one false step for the sake of the man she loved.
She was a professional outcast. She was a woman who
made it her business day by day to sell herself over

the counters of iniquity. She was one of those whose feet in all ages take hold on hell.

So Jephthah had a bad chance. He was the fragment of a home that never was. He had no father that dared to own him. And the first eyes into which he looked were the eyes of an unclean woman. And the first lips that kissed him were lips soiled and stained by years of sinful living. Poor little baby. Poor little foundling. Poor little outcast. How much he missed.

What are the most precious memories in your life to-night? What are the scenes to which you look back with deepest love and tenderness? I know. They are the scenes of your childhood's home.

"How dear to my heart are the scenes of my childhood,
    When fond recollection presents them to view;
  The orchard, the meadow, the deep tangled wildwood,
    And every loved spot that my infancy knew."

But the secret of the fascination of those dear scenes is this, that we saw them by the glow of the light of love. We think tenderly of our early homes because they were presided over by a father and mother who knew God. And the one cord that has failed to snap between us and a good life is the cord that ties us still to the faith of our fathers and our mothers.

But Jephthah missed all this. His father was unfaithful. His mother was an unclean woman. There were no tender and holy associations that made it easy for him to be good. There were no memories to come in after years and whisper old half forgotten prayers. There were no fond recollections to lay their hands upon him with angelic tenderness and lead him away from his City of Destruction. He was a child of sin, a child of blackness and of night, a child bereft of the inspiration of a good mother's life and the sweet uplift of a pious home.

And not only was this man wronged in what he missed, he was equally wronged in what he suffered. Early he was branded with a shame not his own. I know of few places where society has been so unjust and unkind as it has in its condemnation of those innocent ones who are the victims of another's sin. We forget that every child comes into the world with the Father's kiss upon its clean soul regardless of the circumstances of its birth. We forget also that that child is no more to blame for those circumstances than it is to be blamed for the currents of the sea or for the darkness of the night.

But Jephthah was blamed. Ugly names were flung at him before he was old enough to know their dark and sinister meaning. He was forbidden to go to the big house of his father before he knew why he was not allowed to go. He was excluded from the games of those more fortunately born than he, when he could no more understand why he was excluded than he could keep back the bitter tears of childish disappointment. I can see him as he watches his half brothers and sisters play in the distance, and his little heart is lonely and he is hungry for a playmate. And the gate is shut in his face, the gate of a shame not his own.

By and by youthhood comes, and early manhood. The parental estate is to be divided. Jephthah is disinherited. He is driven from among his people. He is forced to flee for his life. And he goes to take refuge in Tob with its mountain fastnesses and with its rude heathens who are less unkind than those kinsmen of his who claim to be worshippers of Jehovah.

So we have here the material out of which this young man is called on to build a life. He has no parentage. He has no kindred. He has no friends. Nobody believes in him. Everybody expects him to go wrong. It seems even at times as if everybody wanted him to go wrong. They said, "Oh, yes, I know him. I used to know his mother. She died in the gutter. You can't expect anything of him."

And it is not at all difficult to go down when everybody expects you to go down. It is a great thing to have somebody to trust you. That is a tremendous help. As long as you feel that there is somebody who counts on you, who believes in you, you are not without an anchor. I read the other day of a little newsboy who was given a quarter that he might get change. And on his way back he was run over and crushed by an auto. And the last word he said was, "Be sure and hunt him up and give him back the change. He trusted me." But here is a young fellow exiled, robbed, persecuted and mistrusted. And out of this charred and ugly material he is called upon to build a life.

And what is the result? Well, he refused to surrender. He said, "If nobody else will believe in me I will believe in myself. Since nobody else will help me, I will help myself. If I am to be robbed of my inheritance I will make a way of my own." And so he set to work. He did not spend his time hunting up his neighbors to tell them of his misfortunes. He did not put in his time boasting of what he would do if he were as well off as his half brothers down in Israel. He went to work to build his fortune in the here and now. And little by little he won.

And then one day a runner came to him in the field

and said, "Jephthah, you have company at your house."
And the man looked up in surprise and said, "Company! Who is it?" "A committee of elders from
Israel." And Jephthah is astonished. He is filled with
wonder. He is trying to guess why they came. And
with the problem unsolved he goes to meet his guests.

These elders greet him like a long lost son. They
tell him how they rejoice in his prosperity. They informed him how they had always known that he would
make good. They let him know that they would never
have sent him out of Israel if they had had their way
about it. And then at last they gather courage to tell
him their errand. And they say, "Israel is being besieged by the Ammonites and we want you to come and
be the commander-in-chief of our armies."

Well, now that was a shock. Here was a young
fellow who began with nothing, and worse than nothing. But instead of whining, instead of quitting, instead of complaining that he had no chance, instead of
putting in his time wishing that he was somewhere
else, he did his duty where he was. And folks found
it out and came to kneel at his feet and ask him for
help. And I am not saying, young man, that every
man gets his just deserts, but I do say that in the overwhelming majority of cases, if a man is really any
account, sooner or later somebody will find it out. It
may be true that

"Full many a gem of purest ray serene
    The dark unfathomed caves of ocean bear.
Full many a flower is born to blush unseen,
    And waste its sweetness on the desert air."

But I doubt if any gem of real human worth ever lies
permanently concealed. I seriously question if any

radiant flower of human character ever wastes its sweetness on the desert air. Learn to do something that the world needs to have done and men will make a path to your door even if you live in a desert.

They came and asked Jephthah for help. It is a humiliating experience. Now, I suppose those half brothers of Jephthah's down in Israel, those fellows who had scorned him in his childhood, those fellows who had robbed him of his share in the estate,—I suppose they did some loud talking about the general being a kinsman of theirs. Oh, they are very much like we are. We seldom boast of our relationship to an outcast, but if we are one hundred and first cousin to somebody who is prominent we are mighty apt to go about telling it.

Jephthah heard their request and promised to help them. I think that was fine of him. It would have been so easy for him to have said, "Oh, yes, you kicked me out when I was a little helpless waif. When I needed help you would not give it. When I needed help you laughed at my childish tears. Now you need help, I will laugh at you." But there was nothing of revenge in him. Wronged as he had been, he would not nurse his wrongs. He would not allow his bitter treatment to make him bitter.

I wish we all were so wise. You were injured years ago by somebody. That somebody perchance was in the church. And so you have never had any use for the church since. You have never had any use much for anybody since. You have been snarling and snapping. Do you remember Miss Harrisham in "Great Expectations"? She was to be married. All arrangements were made. The wedding cake was on the table. But at twenty minutes to nine a cruel note came telling her that the groom was not coming.

Therefore, the clocks were all stopped at twenty minutes to nine. The cake stood upon the table till it rotted. The blinds remained drawn and no sunlight was ever allowed in the house again. And life for her stopped at twenty minutes to nine. One disappointment wrecked her, embittered her, made her throw her life away. But Jephthah refused to be embittered.

He consented to go. But before he undertook the campaign he stood beside the altar of God. This man had lived for years among heathens, but they had not heathenized him. He still stood true by the altar. Circumstances were against him, but religion is not simply for the easy situations in which we find ourselves. Your test, as one has said, is not how good you can be if you have a devoted saint on either side of you down at the office. Your test is what your religion can do for you in the midst of a godless crowd. Daniel's God was tested not in the pleasant situations of his early home life. The test was among his foes. It is amidst the horrors of a lion's den that the king's question echoes, "Oh, Daniel, servant of the living God, is thy God whom thou servest continually, able to deliver thee?"

Jephthah went to battle from the altar of prayer. As he went he made a vow. It is the vow for which he has been most severely criticized. It is a vow that has caused his name among some to be branded with shame. He vowed that if God would give him the victory he would offer to Him whatever first came out of the door of his house to meet him on his return. It was a rash vow, I am ready to admit. Yet rash as it was, I do not find it in my heart to be severely critical of him. I rather join with Dr. Peck in my admiration. You know what is the matter with a great many of

us smug church members? We are so prudent. We
have such admirable possession of all our faculties.
We are in danger of dying of self-control. This man
in the white heat of his enthusiasm made a solemn
pledge to the Lord of that which was destined to be
infinitely the most precious thing in his life. But some
of us in our prudence will not even make a pledge
of a few dollars. We say we do not know how well
we will be fixed next week or next month or next year.

You have heard of the man who subscribed $50 and
refused to pay it, saying that he was too religious that
day to look after his own interests. Some of us never
get that religious. But all the encomiums throughout
the Word of God are uttered upon those who are
utterly rash in their giving. The widow foolishly gave
away all that she had. And Mary squandered a whole
box of ointment when a few drops would have been
amply sufficient. But it was their mad recklessness that
made them immortal.

Jephthah made his vow and went to battle. He
went confidently. He went believing that inasmuch as
he had put himself and what he had at God's disposal,
that God would put Himself at his disposal. And
God did not disappoint him. He won the fight. And
now the victorious army is marching home. The soldiers are rejoicing. But there is a strange tenseness
and anxiety in the general's face that the soldiers do not
understand. Nobody understands but God and Jephthah. At last they round the bend in the road and
the general comes in sight of his own home. And then
suddenly his bronze face goes deadly pale. He reels
upon his horse. For out from the door of his home
has come a lovely girl with dark hair and sunny face,
and she is singing a song of welcome.

Father and daughter come face to face. The girl is perplexed, and the general strains her hard to his heart. He is father and mother to her at once, and she is all he has. And the cup is bitter almost beyond the drinking. And he says, "Alas, my daughter, you have brought me very low." And he tells her his story. And the girl with sweet resignation understands, and the great sacrifice is made.

Jephthah was a hard man, you say. Do not judge him in the light of the twentieth century. Judge him in the light of the day in which he lived. And remember this, that he had the manhood to keep his promise. Remember that he had the sturdy courage to pay his vow. "I have opened my mouth unto the Lord, and I cannot go back." Oh, the world is saved by the "cannot" men, by the men who have big impossibilities in their souls. Joseph says as he faces the temptation of his life, "I cannot do it." The apostles ordered to keep silent, say, "We cannot." And Jephthah with breaking heart and tear-wet face, tempted to break his vow, says, "I cannot go back."

Oh, I know what we would probably have done. We would have said to ourselves, "Nobody knows that I made that vow anyway, nobody but God. I made it in the secrecy of my own heart. I never breathed a word into any human ear. If I go back on it, it will not matter so much. It is simply a promise that I made to God." This man had not told his vow. It was a secret between himself and his Lord. He was not driven to the performance of it by public opinion. He was not urged to it, as flabby Herod, "for the sake of those that sat with him." He was urged to it by his own unstained conscience and his sterling manhood.

Or he might have said, "I made the vow, it's true,

but I made it under pressure. A great danger was threatening and a man is not to be held responsible for a vow he makes in the presence of danger." Did you ever get frightened when a storm was on and promise God things, and then go back on it? Of course you have. We have been false to one another, some of us. How many of us have been false to God! How far is this old hero ahead of ourselves!

Think of the vows that you have made as members of the church. You have not even fulfilled the vow you made to your groceryman. Some of you have not paid for the clothes that you have on, and never will. Some of you have made pledges to the church and have forgotten them. And just because the church won't sue you, you are going to break the promise that you have made, not simply to men, but to God.

And what have you done with your church vows? You have promised to renounce the devil and all his works, the vain pomp and glory of the world. Have you kept your vow? You have promised to obediently keep God's holy will and commandments. Have you been honest with God in this matter? You have promised to be subject to the rules of the church and to attend upon its services, and some of you have trampled on those rules flagrantly, openly, knowingly. And remember that when you took that vow it was not a pledge that you made to me. You opened your mouth that day unto the Lord.

And you that are here outside the church, may the Lord help you to pay your vows unto the Most High. For there is hardly a single one of you but that at some time has opened your mouth unto the Lord. What about that promise you made to God when you were sick? I do not say you made it into any human ear, but you breathed it in prayer into His ear. What about the promise you made to God by the coffin of your baby? What about the promise of consecration you made by the bedside of your dying mother? May the Lord help us to make this day a pay day. May the Lord give us the courage to say, "I have opened my mouth unto the Lord, and I cannot go back."

X

A CASE OF BLUES—ELIJAH

1 *Kings* 19:4

One day you were reading in the New Testament and you came to that surprising word from James: "Elijah was a man subject to like passions as we are." And if you were reading thoughtfully you stared at that sentence in wide-eyed amazement. And then in your heart you said, "It isn't true. Elijah's story doesn't read a bit like mine."

Then you thought of how he came and put his finger in Ahab's face and made that face go white. You thought of how he carried Heaven's key in his pocket for three years and six months. You thought of his lifting the dead boy into life; of his victory on Carmel; of his quiet walk to the little station beyond the Jordan where the Heavenly Limited met him and took him home. And again you felt like saying that James was altogether mistaken.

To fortify yourself more fully you reread his story. Then you came to this passage and you read it with a gasp: "And he came and sat down under a juniper tree," etc. And down by the print of your foot you saw the big footprint of the old prophet and you said, "After all, we are very much alike. After all, he got in the dumps, fretted and broke his heart with the blues, even as I."

Now, what was the matter with Elijah? He was not a natural and deliberate pessimist. There are some folks that are, you know. There are some people who study to be pessimistic. They are the "self-appointed inspectors of warts and carbuncles, the self-elected supervisors of sewers and street gutters." They pride themselves on being guides to the Slough of Despond and on holding a pass key to the cave of Giant Despair.

One such woman, being asked how she felt, said, "I feel good to-day. But I always feel the worst when I feel the best because I know how bad I am going to feel when I get to feeling bad again." Two buckets went to a well one day. One sobbed and said, "Oh, me! it breaks my heart to think that however full we go away from the well, we always come back empty." And its companion laughed outright and said, "Why, I was congratulating myself on the fact that however empty we come to the well, we always go away full."

One morning when the world was brimming with spring, two little girls ran out into a garden where the dewdrops and the sunlight and God had wrought the miracle of a hundred full-blown roses. They looked at the lovely scene and one went back and said tearfully, "Oh, mother, the roses are blooming, but there is a thorn for every rose." The other looked and went back singing and said, "Mother, the roses are blooming and there is a rose for every thorn."

No, this man was not a deliberate pessimist. Had he been his name and memory would have rotted long ago, for the men that bless us are the hopeful men, the forward-looking men. I read of a man who was put in jail during the Boer War simply because he was always prophesying disaster. He was a discourager. He refused to see anything hopeful. And a man of that kind ought to be in jail because he is as harmful as a man with the small-pox. "He who steals my purse steals trash, but he who filcheth from me" my sunny outlook, my expectation of the dawn of a tomorrow, "takes that which not enriches him, but makes me poor indeed."

What was the matter with Elijah? Well, in the first place, he was tired. He was utterly spent. He had just passed through a very trying and exacting ordeal. We can well imagine that the days just preceding the test upon Carmel were toilsome days and the nights were sleepless nights. Then came the great day of contest and victory. There was, of course, no rest that day. And, in the exhilaration of victory, you know how he ran before the chariot of Ahab from Carmel to Jezreel, a distance of seventeen miles.

Arrived there, he got a message from Jezebel threatening his life. He had expected, of course, that the men who had shouted "The Lord He is God" would stand by him. But they did not. He had expected that even Jezebel would be afraid to lift her voice in defense of the old defeated heathenism of the past. But here again he was much mistaken. In fact, instead of tamely acknowledging defeat she sends him this word: "So let the gods do to me, and more also, if I make not thy life as the life of one of them by to-morrow about this time."

Jezebel's threat totally upset the prophet's sense of victory. He came to feel that he had not won after all. For the first time he gave way to fear. Cowardice rushed upon him and drove him, without rest, down the road that led into the wilderness. The terminus of this road was, quite naturally, the juniper tree.

So one source of his discouragement, one secret of his being in the blues, was that he was utterly tired. It is hard indeed for a man to be hope-

ful when his nerves are on edge. It is hard for him
to keep out of the blues when he is completely ex-
hausted. As a tired body yields at such times far
more readily to physical disease, so does it yield more
readily to the exquisite torture of discouragement and
depression.

A second reason for his collapse was a lost sense
of the divine fellowship. Up to this time Elijah's
every step had been ordered of the Lord. He had a
sense of the Divine Presence that was continuous.
But Jezebel's threat had made him believe that he
must look out for himself. So he took his case into his
own hands. And that is the road that must always lead
to the juniper tree.

Such a collapse is next to impossible as long as
we keep on intimate terms with God. Yonder is a
man named Paul on a ship that is going to pieces. The
sea "curls its lips and lies in wait with lifted teeth
as if to bite." The sailors' faces are ghastly with
hunger and panic. But while despair grips every
other heart and while death laughs with hollow laughter amidst the popping timbers of this wrecking ship,
this man steadies himself and shouts, "Be of good
cheer." What is the secret of his cheer? "There stood
by me this night the angel of God whose I am." He
was saved by an intimate and personal sense of the
Divine Presence. Elijah had lost this sense of the
Divine. Hence the deep, dark night of utter discouragement was upon him.

Thus utterly wearied and his old intimacy with
the Lord gone, the worst naturally followed. All his
hopes seemed to fall about him. There came to him
a heart-breaking sense of personal failure. He sobbed
out the complaint: "I am no better than my fathers.

They allowed Israel to drift into idolatry. I have not been able to bring it back. I have accomplished nothing. I toiled long and hard, dreaming that at the end I would clasp the warm, radiant hand of success and victory, but in reality I only clasp the skeleton hand of failure."

Have you ever had a feeling that you were of no account and never would be; that in spite of all that God had done for you, you were a failure? There are few things more fraught with heartache and bitterness and discouragement than that. That is something that makes you want to sob and give over the fight utterly. And there are a lot of folks that allow themselves to come to that dismal conviction. They work, and nobody seems to appreciate it. They toil, and nobody compliments them. Then they decide that they do not amount to anything, and they feel like giving over the fight.

I read the other day a fascinating essay from Frank Boreham. In this essay the author spoke of a certain discouraged friend of his. He declared it his purpose to help this friend by sending him a present. And the strange present that he was going to send him was an onion. Yes, he was going to wrap this onion in lovely tissue paper and put it in a beautiful candy box and tie it with pink ribbon and post it to his friend at once.

Now, why send him an onion? Well, for the simple reason that though an onion is one of the most valuable of all vegetables, though it is the finest of relishes, though it has added piquancy to a thousand feasts, yet nobody praises the onion. Of course you know the author is right here. You may have read some great poetry in your time, poems on daffodils, violets, roses, daisies. Even you have known a great poet who could write about a louse and a field mouse, but where do you find a poem about an onion? What orator waxes eloquent in its praise? What bride ever carries a bouquet of onions as a bridal bouquet?

This is true, of course, but why is it true? Not because the onion is useless. The real reason is because it is so strong. It is harder to grow sentimental over great strong things,—though tears have been shed over onions, as our essayist has pointed out. There are some we praise, you know, because we think that they need it to keep them going. They are weak. There are others we do not praise because they are so strong, or because, being strong, we expect strong things of them. The football hero receives an ovation when he makes a touchdown, but no greater than the baby receives when it takes its first step. There was more noise in the former case, but only because there was a larger crowd of spectators. So it is not wise to conclude that because nobody is praising you, you are of no account in the world.

Not only did Elijah for the moment lose faith in himself, but he lost faith in others as well. He thought there was not a good man in all Israel. And if you want a short cut to wretchedness, get to a place where you do not believe in anybody. Some people seem to cultivate this disposition as if it were an asset. It is not an asset. It is the worst possible liability. If you want to make a hell for yourself in the here and now, cultivate the habit of seeing a selfish motive back of every seemingly unselfish act. School yourself to believe that all men and all women have their price. Say not in haste, but deliberately, that "All men are liars."

That is the leading characteristic of the devil.

"Hast thou considered my servant, Job," the Lord asked, "that there is none like him?" "Yes," replied the devil, "I have considered him. I know him through and through. I know him better than you do. He is deceiving you. He is putting it over on you. You think he loves you for yourself,—I know that he loves you simply because you are feeding him bonbons. Let me touch him and he will curse you to your face." That is the devil's habit. That is what makes him such a success as a devil.

If you do not believe in people no wonder you are miserable. If you do not believe that a fluctuating Simon can be changed into a rock; if you do not believe that a Magdalene can, through the grace of God, become a herald of the resurrection; if you do not believe that this world of men is a salvable world; then it is not to be wondered at that you are blue. If you do not believe in the honesty and goodness and purity of at least a few, I do not see how you can be in any other place than a veritable perdition.

There are bad men, vicious men, godless men, but they are not all so. Do not believe that they are.

> "There are loyal hearts, there are spirits brave;
> There are souls that are good and true,
> Then give the world the best you have
> And the best will come back to you.
>
> "Give love, and love to your heart will flow
> And strength for your utmost need.
> Give faith and a score of hearts will show
> Their faith in your worldly deed.
>
> "Give truth and truth will be paid in kind,
> And honor will honor meet;
> And a smile that is sweet is sure to find
> A smile that is just as sweet.

"For life is the mirror of king and slave;
It's just what we are and do.
Then give the world the best you have
And the best will come back to you."

But if you frown at the world the world is going to frown at you, and if you mistrust it, it will mistrust you. I used to stand as a boy on the river bank on my father's farm and shout at the great rugged cliff across the silver Buffalo River. If I spoke kindly to the grim old cliff, its answer would be in the same kindly tone. If there was harshness and menace in my voice, it came back the same way. And life is a big echo. It speaks to us in the tone of our own voice. It gives us the faith or the unbelief that we ourselves give.

And with faith in self gone and also faith in men, it is not to be wondered at that Elijah requested for himself that he might die. But though he made this request, it is not the real sentiment of his heart. It is not the real Elijah speaking. A man ought never to make an important decision when he is in the blues. He is not himself any more than is a man under the influence of drink. Elijah is not himself here. How do we know? He really doesn't mean what he is saying. How do we know that?

Well, he is requesting for himself here that he might die. Now, if he was really in earnest about dying, Jezebel would have attended to that for him without any prayer on his part, if he had just stayed round Jezreel for a while. The truth of the matter is that the love of life is strong in him. The truth of the matter also is that he still believes somewhat in himself and in God and in men. He is just in the blues now and is not saying what he really believes when he is at his best.

When you get in the dumps and fret and fume and wish you were dead, just stop right there and tell yourself that you are a liar. You do not wish anything of the kind. I heard of a man once who was always threatening to commit suicide. He had a good friend who was a pious man and who was grieved by such threats. But he heard them till he knew they meant nothing, so one day he stepped into this man's room at the hotel, laid an ugly looking revolver down on the dresser and said, "John, old man, you have been threatening to take your own life for some time. I do not want you to do it. It is murder and you will have no chance to repent. I love you as I love myself. For this reason I have decided to kill you. I will live long enough to repent. So get over there at the table and make your will." And the man's face went white and he wanted to wait till to-morrow.

How did God cure this man who was in the blues? First, He used a very commonplace remedy. He put him to sleep. He let him rest. Rest is a very religious thing for a tired man. Now, a man who has overworked himself needs to rest from his work. A lot of blue people need rest from idleness. One big reason they are blue is because they have nothing else to do. God gave this man a rest. That was the first step.

In the second place, He showed him his sin. He showed him where he was wrong and brought him to repentance and thus restored the old relationship of the past. He asked him this question: "What doest thou here, Elijah?" The emphasis is on the "doest." Elijah must have blushed at that question. And he said, "Oh, I am whining. I am complaining. I am trying to keep books, to add up a few columns of figures and test by that as to whether I am a success or a failure."

Now, what the Lord wanted Elijah to learn is just what He wants you and me to learn, that our job in this world is not bookkeeping. It is not for us to try to sum up the amount of good we have done. It is not for us to test whether we have succeeded or whether we have failed. The truth of the matter is that we are not always competent to tell the difference between success and failure. There are some seeming successes that in reality are failures and there are some of the supreme failures that have turned out to be the most glorious successes.

The greatest failure in the eyes of men that was ever made, was the failure on Calvary, and yet it came to pass that the world's darkest night was in reality the mother of its brightest day; that its grimmest desert became its sweetest flower garden. Do not break your heart and tear your hair keeping books.

One of the sanest things I ever heard was spoken by an able preacher who came one day to preach in my town. There was almost nobody out to hear him. And he preached a wonderful sermon and closed with this most sensible word: "I don't know what I have accomplished by coming to this town. I only know that I have come with God in my heart and have done my best. I am not keeping books. God is doing that. Some day on the other side of the River I am going to take down my book and look at it,—God will let me,—and I am going to see just what I accomplished when I came to your town." That is sensible and that is religious.

And so the Lord was saying to Elijah: "It is not

your business to keep books. You do not know how to keep them, in the first place. You added up a column of figures and got zero. I added it up and got 7,000. Yes, there are 7,000 that have not bowed the knee to Baal. You have been a help. You have been an inspiration. You have not been a failure, because you have walked with me." God doesn't fail and the man who walks with him will not fail. He may not accomplish his ambition. He may not realize many of the great hopes of his life, but if he lives in the secret place of the Most High his life will never be a failure.

I read not long ago of a young woman who consecrated her life to God for mission work in India. She was ready for the great enterprise, but just before she was to set sail for that far country, her mother was taken sick with a lingering disease. She had to stay and nurse her for some three years. Then the Angel of Release came and the mother went home.

Preparations were made a second time for her setting out to India. But from a little home in the distant west there came a call for help. A widowed sister of this would-be missionary was sick and there were three little children to be cared for. She went to her sister's bedside. In a short time the sister died and the three little orphans were left on her hands, and the one big hope of her life had to be given up. It seemed strange. It seemed hard. Yet she remained true to the task that lay nearest. At last all three children were able to look after themselves. But by that time she herself was too old to go to her loved mission field.

Then one day one of those orphans for whom she had given up her life's dream put her arms around her neck and told her that she was going to be a missionary and that the field that she had chosen was

India. And in later days the other two told the same story. So they all three went away to India to which she had so longed to go. And as they passed out to the land of her love and her prayers this heroic soul knew that she had not failed. And so God's call to Elijah, to you and to me is to leave off our heart-breaking bookkeeping, to put our hands in His and to resume the journey. And as we go we shall in some way shake off our discouragement as a hampering garment and we shall find ourselves in the sunlight once more. And we shall come to know for ourselves that "Thou wilt keep him in perfect peace whose mind is stayed on Thee."

XI

THE SUPREME QUESTION—THE PHILIPPIAN JAILER

Acts 16:30, 31

"What must I do to be saved?" That question was asked by a startled jailer. He was amidst strange and perplexing happenings. He had just seen wonderful sights. He was being shaken by unfamiliar terrors. For these terrors he sought relief and so he asked this infinitely wise question: "What must I do to be saved?"

But this jailer is not the only man that has ever asked that question. He is not the first man that asked it. This is a universal question. Men of all times and of all climes have asked and sought an answer to this question. The cultured Greeks tried to answer it by building altars to many gods. Then realizing that they had missed it, they sought further by building an altar to "the Unknown God." It was in an effort to answer this question that children were once sacrificed to the fire god, Moloch. And it is the struggle to answer the same question that causes the Indian mother to-day to cast her baby into the Ganges and to come home with empty arms and with an empty heart.

I heard a missionary from the heart of Africa say some years ago that he used to live among the savage tribes of the far interior. They were people of the lowest type. They wore no shred of clothing. But in their wild and barbarous religious dances they would swing round and round till they frothed at the mouth and fell down rigid. It was their way, said the missionary, of asking the supreme question: "What must I do to be saved?"

This was a dramatic moment in this jailer's life. It was a moment big with blessing. Look at the picture. Two strange preachers have come to this Roman city of Philippi. Their preaching has brought them into conflict with the authorities. They are drawn before the magistrates. Their clothing is torn from them and they are severely beaten.

It seems that this would have been shame enough and pain enough, but it was not. They were then turned over to a callous and cruel Roman jailer with the order that he should keep them fast. So he threw them into the inner dungeon and made their feet fast in the stocks. The place was foul and cold and dark. Their backs were lacerated and bleeding. And this was their reward for seeking to bring to men the unsearchable riches of Christ.

Now it was dark enough for these two. But they did not lose heart. First they prayed. I can imagine they prayed secretly and then they prayed aloud. And those people in prison heard the voice of prayer for possibly the first time in their lives. Now, real prayer always makes things different. It brings us a consciousness of God. And so as these men prayed their hearts grew warm and joyous till by and by prayer gives place to praise and they begin to sing.

I have wondered what these people sang that night. It might have been the Twenty-third Psalm. Or they might have sung, "I will bless the Lord at all times. His praise shall continually be in my mouth. My soul shall make her boast in the Lord. The humble shall

hear thereof and be glad." Or the Thirty-seventh
Psalm would have sounded well in the darkness of that
hideous dungeon,—"Fret not thyself because of evil
doers, neither be thou envious against the workers of
iniquity. For they shall soon be cut down like the grass
and wither as the green herb." But I think the most
likely of all is the Forty-sixth: "God is our refuge
and strength, a very present help in trouble. Therefore will we not fear though the earth be removed
and though the mountains be carried into the midst
of the sea."

Whatever they sang it was great singing. I think
the angels opened the windows when they heard it.
I think it made the very heart of our Lord glad.
What a surprise it was to those in that gloomy old
prison. They had heard the walls ring with groans
and shrieks. They had heard bitter oaths in the night,
but songs with the lilt of an irrepressible joy in them
—they had never heard anything like that before.

Now as the melody rang through the gloomy cells
something else happened. The old building seemed to
be shaking with the very power of the music. An
earthquake was on and God took this petty prison in
His hand and shook it as a dicer might shake his dice
box, and all its doors were thrown open and the fetters
were shaken from the feet of those that were bound.
And the old jailer is shaken out of his complacency
and out of his bed and a great terror grips him.

I can see him as he picks himself up and looks
about him in dismay. The doors are open. He is
sure that the prisoners are gone. He knows that his
life will be to pay. He will not face the shame of it.
He will inflict justice upon himself. He draws his
sword and prepares to thrust it through him, but

Paul's eyes were upon him, and knowing his purpose he shouts at him, "We are all here, Jailer. Do thyself no harm."

There is love in that cry, tenderness in it, longing in it that the jailer could not understand. Neither could he fail to realize the might of it. It touches him deeply. He is gripped by another terror, the terror that has come through the presence of these strange men who have brought the things of eternity to seem real to him. And urged on by that new terror he rushes to these men of bleeding backs and tattered garments and throws himself at their feet with this great question in his heart and upon his lips, "Sirs, what must I do to be saved?"

Now, I am aware of the fact that this jailer was a heathen and I am not accusing him at all of being a great theologian. I do not know how learned he was. I do not know whether he could read or write or not. I do not know whether he was widely traveled or not. He may have never been beyond the precincts of his own city. But what I do know is this, that he asked the biggest question that ever fell from human lips. There can be no greater. It was the greatest for him. It is the greatest for you. It is the greatest for me. "What must I do to be saved?" There is no question quite so big as that.

And I am wondering now if it is a big question to you. Remember, it is not: What must I do to be decent? It is not: What must I do to be respectable? These things are all right, but they are not supreme. It is not: What must I do to get rich? Millions of us are asking that question as if it were the one question of eternal importance. But you know that it is not. It is not: What must I do to be beautiful? Some of us are asking that question too, and some of us, I am sorry to say, are missing the answer to it very much. But that is not the big question. The supreme question is: "What must I do to be saved?"

What is implied in this question when it is asked intelligently? There is implied, first of all, that there is an absolute difference between being saved and lost. There is implied in it that there are two classes of people, not the cultured and the uncultured, not the learned and the unlearned. They are the saved and the lost. They are those that have life and those that do not have life.

I am perfectly aware that we of to-day do not like such dogmatic divisions. But I call your attention to the fact that they are the divisions that are made in the New Testament. They are the divisions that Jesus made. He puts folks into two classes, and only two. There were two gates, one was broad and the other narrow. There were two foundations on which a man might build, one was of sand and the other of rock. Mark you, He did not divide men into the perfect and the imperfect, but into those that had life and those that did not have it. And it was He that said, "He that hath the Son hath life, and he that hath not the Son hath not life." So this question, if it means anything, means that there is such a thing as being saved and there is such a thing as being lost. That fact is recognized throughout the entire Bible.

This question implies, in the second place, a consciousness of being lost. "What must I do to be saved?" When this man asked that question there were many things about which he was uncertain. He was uncertain as to how he was to get out of his darkness. He was uncertain as to how he was to be saved, but of one thing he was sure—he was dead sure that he was lost. He did not try to dodge that fact. He did not shut his eyes to it. He did not try in any way to deny it.

And, if you are here without God I hope you will not deny it. For if you have not taken Jesus Christ as your personal Savior you are lost. Then the best thing you can do, the first step to be taken in the direction of getting saved, is to realize your lostness. A man will not send for the physician unless he believes himself sick. He will not try to learn unless he realizes his ignorance. Neither will he turn to God for salvation unless he realizes that he is lost. Oh, it is a good day for a man when he gets a square look at himself. It is a great day when he has a glimpse of himself as God sees him. It is a great hour when, conscious of his guilt, he bows himself in the presence of Him who alone can save and says, "God, be merciful unto me a sinner."

This question implies, in the third place, not only that the man is lost who asked it, but that there is a possibility of his being saved. "What must I do to be saved?"—and here was a man conscious of being lost, conscious of being sin scarred and stained and guilty, yet he believes, and he is right in believing, that salvation is possible for him. He believes that even he can be saved unto the uttermost. There is such a thing as salvation and it is possible for me, even me, to lay hold of it.

And you too must realize that, otherwise it will do you no good to realize the fact that you are a sinner. It is not enough to know yourself lost. You must also believe that you may be saved. It is not enough to realize that you are weak; you must believe that it is possible for you to be strong. You must believe that even a fluctuating Simon can be made into a rock. You must believe in the power of God to remake men, otherwise for you the question is only a question of black despair.

This question implies, in the fourth place, a willingness to be saved. "What must I do to be saved?" This man is not asking this question to gather material for a future argument. He is no speculator. He is no trifler. He is not even asking it because he is intellectually curious. He is not simply asking that he may know the conditions of salvation. He is asking with the earnest purpose in his heart to meet those conditions.

This question implies, in the fifth place, that while salvation is a possibility for you, you must do something in order to obtain it. "What must I do to be saved?" What sort of an answer would you expect to a question like that? What did the apostle say? Did he say, "Do nothing. Let the matter alone. Forget it. Drift?" That is what many of us are doing. No, sir, he said nothing of the kind. He told this man to do something. And this man knew, as you and I know, that if we are ever saved we have got to do something in order to get saved.

I say every one of us knows that, and yet too few of us act as if it were really true. We seem to think that salvation is something that we are going to stumble upon by accident. We seem to think it is something that we are going to receive with absolutely no effort on our own part. We act as if we thought it might be slipped into our pockets while we sleep or dropped into our coffins when we die. Ask the question intelligently, heart,—"What must I do to be saved?" Then you will realize that you must do something.

This question implies, in the next place, that the conditions of salvation are not optional; that it is not up to you and it is not up to me to decide just what we will do in order to be saved. You can accept salvation or you can refuse it. You can meet the conditions or you can refuse to meet them. But one thing you cannot do. You cannot decide upon the terms upon which you will surrender. If you are saved at all you must surrender unconditionally.

So the question is, "What *must* I do to be' saved?" It is not, What is the expedient thing or what is the respectable thing or what is the popular thing to do in order to find salvation? The conditions are not of your choosing and they are not of mine. God has made them and you and I dare not change them. Therefore, if you are ever saved there is not something simply that you ought to do, but there is something that you absolutely must do.

Last of all, this question implies that salvation is an individual matter. "What must *I* do?" It is not a question of what must God do. He has made full provision for the salvation of the whole world. It is not what must the Church do. It is not what must the preacher do. It is not what must this man that is beside me and this man that is behind me or in front of me do. The question comes to my own heart— "What must *I* do?"

"What must I do to be saved?" You must do something, but there are many things that we are doing that will not save us. If you expect to be saved, in the first place, do not depend on your own goodness. "All your righteousnesses are but as filthy rags." Do not count on your own decency. No man was ever saved that way. I challenge you to find one single one. I was holding a meeting some years ago and I met a young fellow who told me he was good enough without Jesus Christ. Of course he was not saved. A man who says that virtually tells Christ that He has misunderstood his case altogether and that Calvary was a wasted tragedy so far as he himself is personally concerned.

Neither will you be saved trusting in the other man's badness. I know what some of you are saying to yourselves as I preach. You are telling yourselves one of the oldest lies that was ever told. You are saying, "I would be a Christian but there are so many hypocrites in the Church." How many men give that as a reason, but it is no man's reason. And I never knew one man to be saved by it. Believe me, the shortcomings and the sins of my brother are mighty poor things to depend on for my own personal salvation.

Again, you will not be saved by seeking an easy way. You will never win by catering to your own pride and cowardice. I was conducting a revival in a Texas city some years ago. At the close of one of the services a young lady came forward to shake hands with the preacher. As she did so she said, "I am going to become a Christian." I congratulated her upon her decision, but she answered, "Oh, I do not mean right now. I mean I am going to be very soon."

"You see," she continued, "it is like this: I am going in a few days to visit some of my relatives that live way back in the country. There is going to be a revival nearby. It will be easy for me to make the decision there because nobody knows me. But here it is different. Everybody knows me here and I simply haven't the courage to come out and take an open stand for Jesus Christ." She went into the country as she planned but she was not saved. Of course not. Nobody ever found salvation by catering to his own cowardice and pride and seeking an easy way.

"What must I do to be saved?" There is an answer to this question. It is an answer that is absolutely dependable. There is nothing in all the world of which I am more sure than I am of the correctness of the answer to this question. I am as sure of it as I am of my own existence. I am as sure of it as I am of the fact of God.

I wonder if you are interested to know the answer. Remember that it is the answer to your supreme question. It is the answer to the most important question that was ever asked. It is the most important that you will ever be called to act upon in this world. Does the prospect of an answer quicken your heartbeat? Does it shake you out of your lethargy into intensest interest? It ought to if it does not. For the answer that I give is not the answer of a mere speculator or dreamer. It is the answer of inspiration and it is an answer whose truth has been tested by the personal experience of countless millions. "What must I do to be saved?" Answer: "Believe on the Lord Jesus Christ and thou shalt be saved."

What is it to believe on the Lord Jesus Christ? It is to believe that Jesus Christ can do what He claims to do and what He has promised to do and to depend on Him to do it. Mr. Moody tells us how that he was in his cellar one day when he looked up and saw his little girl making an effort to see him. She could not because it was dark in the cellar. "Jump," said Mr. Moody, "Daddy will catch you." And instantly the little girl jumped. Now, that was faith.

That was believing on her father. So the jailer believed on the Lord Jesus Christ. He depended upon Him then and there for salvation.

And what happened? He was saved. That very moment Christ came into the man's heart and he became a new creation. He became possessed of a new joy. He became possessed of a new tenderness.

Did you notice what he did? He took water and washed the stripes of the preachers. Paul and Silas were bleeding when they came to the prison but the jailer did not care. But now that he had found Christ he has already begun to be a partaker of the divine nature. A new love has come to him. He has become tender where he was cruel before. Even so does the power of Jesus Christ make men over.

Now, this question: do you want to be saved? If you do you can be. It is the surest thing in all the world. It is as sure as the fact that night follows day. It is more sure than the fact that if you sow wheat you will reap it, that if you believe on the Lord Jesus Christ you shall be saved. Test the matter now and you will know the blessed fact in your own experience.

XII

THE MOTHER-IN-LAW—NAOMI

It is thoroughly refreshing to come upon this exquisite bit of literature called "Ruth." It follows, as you know, immediately after the bloodstained stories we read in Judges. It shows that while there was war and confusion and hate there was also friendship and love and romance. It is a bit of exquisite beauty elbowed on either side by ugliness. This delightful story comes to us like a glad surprise. It is like finding a spring bubbling up in the desert. It is like plucking roses amidst ice bergs. It is like finding a violet in the very crater of a volcano.

I hope you have read the Book of Ruth and are familiar with it. If you haven't you have slighted one of the sweetest and tenderest stories ever told. If you haven't you have neglected about the most delicate and winsome idyl to be found in ancient or modern literature. I have read some good literature, first and last. I have read poetry that lifted the heart and "set the soul to dreaming." I have read prose strong as granite and songful as a mountain brook. But I confess to you, if I wanted to find a finer piece of literature than the book of Ruth, I would be at a great loss to know where to search.

The author sets you down at once amidst strange scenery. And the characters, while genuinely human, are also full of the witchery of romance and poetry. Here is the story. The rains have failed in the Beth-

140

lehem country and the harvests have been exceedingly meager. A certain little family composed of husband, wife and two children, is having a hard fight to keep the wolf from the door. Elimelech, the husband, can find no work and Naomi, the wife and mother, "kneads hunger in an empty bread tray," and goes through the daily torture of being asked for bread that she is not able to supply.

Then one dark day the husband comes home utterly discouraged. He takes up the discussion where it was left off the day before. "Yes," he says, "there is nothing else to do. There is no bread in the land. There has been rain in Moab. We can go there. I do not know how they will receive us, but at any rate, they can only kill us and that is better than starvation."

And Naomi's sad face becomes a shade sadder and she says, "The will of the Lord be done. But I had so hoped that we might be able to remain in the land of our fathers. You see, my dear, it is not of myself that I am thinking. We have two boys. We do not want to rear them in Moab. Moab, I know, is not far off physically, but it is a long way morally. If we go there we may lose our children. The time may even come when they will break the law of Moses and marry among the Moabites."

But, hard as it was for her to consent, at last she was driven into it by sheer starvation. And we see the pathetic little family scourged by hollow-eyed hunger from the land of their fathers into the land of the heathen Moabites. Just what their reception was there we are not told. However, I am quite sure that they were received more kindly than they had expected. Their want and their own kindness seemed to have opened the hearts of the strangers among whom they went to live. Certain it is that the husband and father was able to find sufficient work to keep from actual starvation. By and by times grew better. The pinch of poverty let up, and they began to feel somewhat at home in the land of their adoption.

But the boys were playing with the children of the Moabites. Of course they were. All children are alike. They know no barriers of kindred, of class or of religion. A child is the true democrat. Sad to say, we soon train him out of this. But he is a thorough democrat by nature. He plays as gladly with the son of a scrub woman as with the son of a queen. He lavishes his love as freely upon a pickaninny as upon a prince. So these Jewish boys were playing with the heathen children.

Then a few years went by and the pious father and mother came to realize with horror that their two boys were actually in love with two Moabitish girls. Not only did they love them, but they even wanted to marry them. This was a calamity indeed. I can hear the protests of the father and mother. They warn them of the danger of such marriages. They plead the law of Moses. But all in vain. And we are not surprised. You might as well get in front of Niagara Falls and say "Boo!" and expect it to flow back the other way, as to try to reason with the average young fellow who is in love. Both boys married Moabitish women.

And then what did this wise and godly father and mother do? They did not do what is so usual in cases of an unwelcome marriage. Our boy or our girl makes what seems to us a foolish and ruinous marriage. Then what do we do? We declare that we will never speak to them again, that they shall never darken our doors. And we thereby help on a disaster that might never have come. Naomi and her husband had better sense. They took the wives of their two sons, heathens though they were, into their home and into their hearts. They felt sure that that was the one way that promised a remedy.

Then one day disaster came to the little home of the strangers. The husband and father died, and Naomi was left with the whole responsibility of the family upon her lone shoulders. Her daughters-in-law had seen her in her joy. They marked her also in her sorrow. They were impressed, no doubt, by her calmness and her strength. She walked with the sure and quiet step of one who felt underneath her and round about her the Everlasting Arm.

Then the final disaster came. Both the boys died. Naomi was not only a widow, but she was childless. There were now no bonds that held her longer from the land of her fathers. She decides, therefore, to return. Her two daughters-in-law are to accompany her as far as the border of Moab. There they are to bid her farewell and then go each her own way. They make the journey, these three women, to the borders of Moab. Here Orpah tells Naomi good-bye. She parts from her with real grief and regret, for she loves her genuinely. I think I can hear her sobbing as she takes her lone way back to her own people.

Then it is Ruth's time to say good-bye. I see her as she flings her arms about the neck of Naomi and there she clings. "There, there," says the older woman, "you must be gone now. Your sister is going. She will turn the bend of the road in a minute. Go after her and God grant that you may find rest each in the house of her husband."

But Ruth clings only the tighter. And then she

makes a confession. It is a confession of love. And nothing finer in point of tenderness and beauty was ever uttered by human lips. I hope you are not too old to thrill over a love story. John Ridd's devotion to Lorna Doone still stirs my heart. And there is the confession of a heroine in another story that we can never forget. "Tell him I never nursed a thought that was not his; that daily and nightly on his wandering way pour a woman's tears. Tell him that even now I'd rather work for him, beg with him, walk by his side as an outcast, live on the light of one kind smile from him, than wear the crown that Bourbon lost."

That is a beautiful confession. It is made by a woman to a man. But this was made by a woman to a woman. And strangest of all, it was made by a daughter-in-law to a mother-in-law. Ruth has this distinction, if none other, that she loved her mother-in-law. Her mother-in-law, mind you, that creature who has been the butt of evil jokes in all languages; the one who has proved the dynamite for the wrecking of not a few homes. This confession is the confession of a daughter-in-law to a mother-in-law.

It is the confession of youth to age. It is spring-time clinging to winter. It is June flinging its arms in a passionate tenderness around the neck of November. "It is time you were going," said Naomi. And Ruth's arms clung all the closer and this exquisite bit of poetry fell from her lips, "Entreat me not to leave thee, or to return from following after thee: for whither thou goest, I will go; and where thou lodgest, I will lodge: thy people shall be my people and thy God my God: where thou diest, will I die, and there will I be buried: the Lord do so to me, and more also, if aught but death part thee and me."

You cannot beat that. No confession of love has ever surpassed it. But it is more than a confession of love. It is also a confession of faith. It is the declaration of a strong woman's choice. As Ruth clings to the woman she loves she announces her decision, a decision to which she remained true through all the future years. "Thy people shall be my people and thy God my God."

And the people of the little village of Bethlehem had something interesting to talk about a few days later. Two strange women had come their way, women who were poverty-stricken and homeless. One of them was a Jewess. The other was a Gentile. Neither of them was welcome. Naomi had lost her place in the life of the community. Ruth, the Moabitess had never had any place.

The days that immediately followed their arrival were sad and bitter days. But the younger woman, with a fine courage, refuses to be a burden. Instead, she will be the support of the mother of her dead husband. So she takes upon herself the menial task of a gleaner. It is harvest time and she goes out into the fields to glean.

Now, it happens in the good providence of God, that the field in which she went to glean belonged to a very rich and prosperous man named Boaz. And to that very field where Ruth was gleaning Boaz came that day. He was a young, vigorous, and positive man. He was accustomed to command. There was a dignity about him that made him seem older than his years. Everybody respected him. He was just and generous and religious.

No sooner was he among the workers than his attention was attracted by the winsome young stranger from

Moab. I do not know why he should notice her at once, but I have a fancy that Ruth was attractive, that she had personality and charm. I feel confident that she had that superior beauty that is born of superior character. Anyway, the great landlord saw her and was interested. And he spoke kindly to her, and when Ruth got home that evening she had an interesting story to tell.

And Naomi—wasn't she interested? I can see the flush of her face and the sparkle of her eye across the centuries. She is a woman, too, every ounce of her. And being a woman, she is by instinct and by nature a match maker. She guesses at once what is going on in the hearts of these two young people. And she sets about with delicate good sense to help them to understand each other. By her wise advice things turn out just as they ought to turn out, and . . . "they lived happy ever after."

Who is the heroine of this exquisite story? I know that first place is given to Ruth. And I am in no sense disposed to try to put her in an inferior position. She cannot be honored too highly. She is so absolutely lovable. But I am going to give first place to Naomi. I do not do this because she is more winsome than Ruth. I do it because she accounts for Ruth. If it had not have been for Naomi, Ruth would have lived and died a heathen in the land of Moab.

Now, what are some of the lessons that we learn from the beautiful life of this ancient woman, Naomi? Were we privileged to sit down beside her in the Father's house to-day, she could teach us many wonderful lessons. But one truth she would impress upon us would be this: that life's greatest losses may, through the grace of God, become its richest gains. She would tell you then of the black despair of those days when she was being driven from her home by the cruel hand of poverty. She would not hesitate to say that it was very difficult for her to keep up faith in God in those dark days. "But the Lord was sending me then to find Ruth. You know He had to have her. The world could not keep house without her at all. Yet I would never have found her but for my terrible poverty."

Then, I think she would tell how she was beginning to feel at home in Moab. "My life was taking root in that foreign soil. I was about making up my mind to live my life there. Then death came. One by one I buried my loved ones till not one of my own flesh and blood was left. Then it was that I resolved to come back home. It was my bitter loss that sent me back. I would never have come back but for that. And had I not come back the marriage of Ruth with its blessed outcome would never have been possible."

This woman learned the fine art of capitalizing her calamities. In the midst of all her poverty and heartache she kept firm her faith in God. And she came thus to realize the sufficiency of His grace. She came to know, even in that distant day, the truth of Paul's great word, "All things work together for good to them that love God." There are times, I know, that it is hard for us to believe this, just as there were times when it was hard for Naomi to believe it. But there came a day when she was privileged to know the truth of it in her own experience. And if you cling to your faith you, too, will come to know, if not here, then by and by.

Then we learn from Naomi, as another has pointed out, the power for blessing that may be in one consecrated life. Naomi was a very hidden and obscure woman. Had you walked by her side as, hunger driven, she left her native land, she would not have told you anything of the great destiny that was ahead. She never dreamed of enriching the world as she did. It never occurred to her that she was to be one of the great light bringers of all the centuries. And yet such was to be the case. The world simply could not get on without Naomi. It could not for the simple reason that Naomi led Ruth into the knowledge of God and into the fellowship of the people of God.

"Thy people shall be my people and thy God my God." That is Ruth's confession of faith. How did she come to make it? How did this lovely heathen ever come to fall in love with Naomi's people? She had never even seen them. She made up her mind, however, that they were the people, of all others, that were most worth knowing. She made up her mind that they must be very winsome and very lovable people. How did she come to that conclusion? Answer: By association with her mother-in-law. That is also how she came to fall in love with God. She was led to the realization of the charm of Him through the God-possessed personality of Naomi.

So it was Naomi who won Ruth to God. It was Naomi who made possible Ruth's successful marriage. Then one day the sweet angel of sufferng came to the home where the one-time-stranger lived and Ruth held her first-born in her arms. And the years went by and there was another child born among the Judean hills and the sunshine was tangled in his hair and countless songs were pent up in his heart. And he so sang and battled and sinned and repented that everybody loved him and we thank God still for David. And David was Ruth's grandbaby.

Then other years went by and there was a burst of light upon those Judean hills. And there was music from a choir that came from that country where everybody sings. "There were shepherds abiding in the fields, keeping watch over their flocks by night. And the angel of the Lord came upon them and the glory of the Lord shone round about them and they were sore afraid. And the angel said, 'Fear not, ye, for behold, I bring you glad tidings of great joy which shall be to all the people; for there is born unto you this day, in the city of David, a Savior who is Christ the Lord.' " And that Savior was another one of Ruth's grandbabies.

But in the purpose of God, neither David nor David's Greater Son would have been possible without Naomi. And so one woman remaining true to God became a roadway along which the Almighty walked to the accomplishment of His great purpose, even the salvation of the world.

XIII

CONFESSIONS OF A FAILURE—THE BUSY MAN

1 *Kings* 20:40

In 1 Kings 20:40 you will find the text. "As thy servant was busy here and there, he was gone." This is part of a parable that was spoken by a certain prophet to King Ahab. This prophet was seeking to rebuke the king for his leniency in dealing with Benhadad, whom he had overcome in battle. It is not our puropse, however, to discuss this parable in relation to its context. We are going to consider it altogether apart from its surroundings. We will rather study it as it is related to ourselves. Here then, is the story of this man's failure from his own lips. "Thy servant went out into the midst of the battle; and, behold, a man turned aside and brought a man unto me, and said, Keep this man: if by any means he be missing, then shall thy life be for his life, or else thou shalt pay a talent of silver. And as thy servant was busy here and there, he was gone."

I imagine I meet this soldier immediately after he has been put in charge of his important captive. He walks with the purposeful stride of one who knows his task and who is setting seriously about doing it. He seems to appreciate the honor that has been conferred upon him. He seems also to have a sense of the serious responsibilities involved. And when he takes his position before the cell of his prisoner he watches with all diligence.

But when I pass his way again next day I am greatly shocked. My soldier is no longer on guard. Another had taken his place. And when I look about for the important prisoner that has been captured at the price of blood and conflict he is no longer to be seen. Upon inquiry I find that he has escaped. In his place, bowed down with shame and dressed in chains, is the man who yesterday was a guardsman.

I cannot pass him by without a question. "How did this come about?" I ask. "Were you surprised and overcome? Did your fellow soldiers allow a strong company to break through their lines and to overpower you and take your prisoner from you? Did a strong hand strike you down from behind in the dark? How is it that your prisoner had escaped?"

And the man, without being able to look me in the eye, answers, "No, he did not escape because I was overpowered. He did not escape because I was surprised. He escaped because I was too busy to watch him." "Too busy," I answer in amazement, "too busy doing what? What task did you find more important than saving your country and saving your own home and saving your own honor?" "Oh, no task in particular," he answers. "I was just busy here and there." That is his confession. "As thy servant was busy here and there, he was gone."

And the man is sentenced to death. And we must admit that the sentence is just. Not that he has committed any aggressive crime. He has not cut anybody's throat. He has not stabbed anybody in the back. He has not stolen anything. He is not being punished for what he has done. He is being punished for what he has failed to do.

And that kind of sin, let me warn you, is just as

dangerous and just as killing as positive and aggressive sin. How foolish are they who think they are pious simply because they do no wrong. How absurd it is to get it into your minds that a man is a Christian by virtue of what he does not do instead of by virtue of what he does. Now, I know that there are certain sins that are damaging and damning, but in order to be lost now and ever more it is not necessary to be guilty of any of them. All that is necessary is that you do what this man did, and that is fail in your duty.

This is what our Lord taught us again and again. What was wrong with the fig tree that He cursed it? It was not loaded with poison. It simply had nothing but leaves. What charge is brought against Dives? No charge at all. We are simply made to see him neglect the man at his gate who needed his help. He does not drive the man away. He simply lets him alone. And over his neglected duty he stumbles out into a Christless eternity. What was wrong with the five foolish virgins? It was not that they had water in their lamps. It was simply the fact that they had no oil. What was the matter with those to whom the judge said, "Depart from me"? Only this, they had failed in their duty. The charge is, "Inasmuch as ye did it not."

So this man failed in his duty. That is what wrecked him. Why did he fail? First, he did not fail through ignorance. He did not fail because he did not know his duty. He understood perfectly what he was to do. He understood also the great importance of his doing it. He knew it was a life and death business with him. I know that he failed. He failed miserably. He failed to his own ruin. But it was not because of his ignorance. And that is not the secret of your failure. We need to know more, all of us, but our greatest need in the moral realm is not for more knowledge. Our greatest need is the will to live up to what we already know. The reason you are selfish, the reason you are unclean, the reason you are godless is not because you do not know better. You have known better through all these years. It is because you are unwilling to do better.

There is not a man here that does not know enough to do his duty. It may be that you do not know the exact niche that the Lord wants you to fill. It may be that you do not know the exact task to which He is calling you. But you do know this, you know that there is an absolute difference between right and wrong, and that you ought to be enlisted on the side of the right. You know that it is your part to help and not to hinder, to bless and not to curse, to lift up and not to drag down.

And while you may not know your particular task, yet it is your privilege to know even that. I am confident that God has a particular task for every single soul of us. And I am equally confident that He will let us know what that task is if we will only make it possible for Him to do so. He tells us how we may know. "In all thy ways acknowledge Him and He shall direct thy path."

There are many misfits in the world, and you know a misfit is the cheapest and most useless thing known. If you want a cheap suit of clothes go to the misfit establishment. I remember when I was a young fellow just getting grown I decided to quit wearing the crude hand-me-down suits such as I could purchase at the village store. I decided that I must have a genuine tailored suit.

So with this idea in mind I wrote for the catalogue of Montgomery Ward & Company. I might have used Sears Roebuck, but I liked Montgomery Ward better. I found the suit I wanted, read his directions, took my own measure and ordered the suit. In due time it came. And I pledge you my word that you might have tried that suit on every form of man and beast that the whole Roman Empire could furnish and it would not have fit a single one of them. The legs of the pants were large enough to keep house in. They would have made admirable wheat sacks, but as trousers they were a failure. To me the suit was worthless because it was a misfit.

And there are many men just as worthless to-day. But they need not have been so. If they did not know their task they might have known it. They did not fail, as this man did not fail, through ignorance.

Second, this man did not fail for lack of ability. If he could have said that he was overpowered, if he could have told that superior numbers came upon him and took his prisoner in spite of himself we could have pardoned him. Or if he could have shown us a scarred breast and a face that had been hacked by a sword, and said, "I won these wounds trying to keep my prisoner," we would have respected him. We would have sympathized with him. But he had no scars to show. He had made no fight at all. Therefore he could not say, "I failed, 'tis true, but I could not help it." Neither can you say that. No man here is failing for lack of ability.

Now, I do not mean by that that you can do anything that you want to do. When I was a boy people used to come to our school and tell us such rubbish as that. But it is all false. Suppose I were to take a

notion to be a great painter, not one after the fashion
of the ordinary sixteen year old girl of to-day, but a
painter like Turner. Why, I might work at it a thousand years and never accomplish anything.

Suppose some of you were to take a notion to be
great singers. Is there any use for me to tell
you that if you persist you will succeed? Not
a bit of it. You might succeed in ruining the nerves
of your teacher. You might easily make those who
hear you practise "want to gnaw a file and flee into
the wilderness." But you would never learn to sing.
There is no hope for some of us till we get to Heaven.

No, we cannot do anything that we might want to
do. But we can do something infinitely better. We
can do everything that God wants us to do. I cannot
do your task, and you cannot do mine. I am glad
that that is true. I am glad that we all do not have
the same aptitudes. I am glad that we all cannot do
successfully the same things. I am glad that we do
not all have the same tastes. But while that is so,
every man has the ability, through grace, to perform
the task to which he is called.

In the third place, this man did not fail because of
idleness. He did not fail because he was lazy. Of
course idleness will wreck anybody. Laziness is a
deadly sin unless it is overcome. I know something
about it because I have had to fight it all my life.
But this man was not an idler. This man was a worker.
He failed, but he did not fail because he refused to
put his hand to any task or to bend his back under
any load.

Why then did this man fail? Not from ignorance,
not from inability, not from idleness. He was busy.
That is his word about himself. And nobody denies

it. "As thy servant was busy here and there, he was gone." What, I repeat, was the secret of his failure? Just this, that though he was busy, he was not busy at his own task. He was simply busy here and there. He was one of those unfortunate souls that has so many things to do and so many engagements to keep and so many functions to attend and so many burdens to carry that he cannot do his own duty.

Do you know of anybody like that? "Did you keep your prisoner?" I ask. "No, I was too busy." "Busy at what, in Heaven's name! Do you know of anything more important than obeying the orders of your king? Do you know of anything more important than helping to save your nation? Do you know of anything of more importance than saving your own life, your own honor, your own soul."

You can see his trouble. He allowed the secondary to so absorb him that he neglected the primary. Those things that he was working at here and there, those unnamed tasks that he was performing, there is no hint that they were vicious things. I am sure that they were altogether harmless. They may have been altogether good and useful. But the trouble with that good was that it robbed him of the privilege of doing the best. The trouble with the Prodigal in the Far Country was not simply the fact that he was in a hog pen. He might have been in a palace and been quite as bad off. It was the fact that he was missing the privilege of being in his Father's house.

The sin that I fear most for many of you is not the sin of vicious wrong-doing. It is the sin of this man, the sin of choosing the second best. I read recently of an insane man who spent all his time in an endeavor to sew two pieces of cloth together.

But the thread he used had no knot in the end of it. So nothing was ever accomplished. Now, there is no harm in such sewing. But the tragedy of it is that if we spend all our time doing such trivial things we rob ourselves of the privilege of doing something better. And that is just the trouble of much of our life to-day. Many of us are engaged in a great, stressful, straining life of trivialities. Some of these are not especially harmful. But the calamity of it all is that they so absorb us that we have no time left for the highest.

Down in Tennessee near where I used to live a house was burned one day. The mother was out at the well doing the week's washing. The flames were not discovered till they were well under way. Of course when they were discovered the woman was seized with terror. She rushed into the house and brought out a feather bed and a few quilts. But in her madness she forgot her own baby and the child was burned to death. Now, I submit to you that there was absolutely no harm in saving a feather bed. There was no harm in saving a few old quilts. The tragedy was that in the absorption of saving all these half worthless things she lost the primary. In her interest in the good she became utterly blind to the best.

I wonder if that is not your folly. You are busy here and there. You go to work six days in the week. You are passionately in earnest about amusing yourself. You do a thousand and one decent and respectable things. But while you are busy here and there the peace of God slips out of your life. While you are busy here and there you neglect the Sunday School and the Church. While you are busy here and there you lose your interest in the Word of God and you forget "the secret stairway that leads into the Upper Room."

"Busy here and there" you lose the sense of God out of your life. "Busy here and there" you allow the altar in your home to fall down. "Busy here and there" you allow your sons and daughters to stumble over that broken down altar into lives of Christless indifference.

Oh, men and women, there is but one remedy for us if we would avoid the rock upon which this condemned guardsman wrecked himself. We must put first things first. Let us listen once more to the voice of the sanest man that ever lived. This is His message: "Seek ye first the kingdom of God and His righteousness, and all these things will be added unto you." If you fail to do this, however noble may be the task at which you toil, life for you will end in tragedy. If you do this, however mean and obscure may be your task, life for you will end in eternal joy and victory.

XIV

A MOTHER'S REWARD—JOCHEBED

Exodus 2 : 9

"Take this child away and nurse him for me and I will give thee thy wages." This text refers to one of the big events of human history. This is one of the most stupendous happenings that was ever recorded. I doubt if there was ever a battle fought that was so far reaching in its influence. I doubt if all the fifteen decisive battles of the world taken together were of greater importance than this event that took place here on the banks of the Nile.

It is a simple story. An Egyptian princess, with her attendants, has come to the riverside for a bath. To her amazement she discovers a strange vessel lying at anchor upon the waters of the river. Her curiosity is aroused. When the vessel is brought to land its cargo is discovered. And what a cargo it is. It is so wonderful, it is so amazingly great that we marvel that any ship should be large enough to hold it. We are amazed that any sea should be vast enough to float such a vessel.

What was this cargo? It was a baby, a baby boy. He is waving dimpled hands and kicking chubby feet, and he is crying. And the vessel upon which he sails becomes a battleship. He at once begins to lay siege to the heart of the princess. He pelts her with his tears. He pierces her through and through with his winsome weakness. He cannonades her with his lovely

159

helplessness till she capitulates and gathers him in her arms. And this princess is no wicked woman, I am sure of that. She had a mother heart. I think I can hear her across the centuries talking to this little waif. She hugs him close. "Yes, yes," she said. "You shall be my baby. The big, old soldiers shan't have you. They shan't kill mother's little boy." And she loved him as her own.

Now, two bright eyes had been witnessing this wonderful scene. There was a little girl hidden nearby and she watched all that happened. And when she saw the princess take her little baby brother to her heart she understood. She felt sure at once that the baby was safe. And a glad and daring thought took possession of her and she hurried from her place of hiding and approached the princess. And this is her word, "My lady, may I get a nurse for your baby?"

And the princess did not despise the little girl. I feel perfectly confident that the spirit of God was moving upon the heart of this princess. She listened to the child and accepted her services. And I can see that little girl as with flying feet she hurries to her mother with the good news. "Mother, they have found Little Brother, but they are not going to kill him. The Princess found him and I told her that I would get somebody to nurse him for her. Come, and we may have him for our own again."

Now, I take it that it was an important event when the Princess decided that the child was to live. The death sentence had gone out against him. You know that. The death sentence had been pronounced against every son of the Hebrews. But an even more important event took place when the Princess decided who should be the baby's nurse. When she decided who should

have the training of the child, then she decided what
the child was to be. Suppose, for instance, she had
determined to train him herself, she would have made
him like herself. Moses would have become a heathen
in spite of the blood in his veins. He was destined
to be a genius, but his genius might have been very
far from being the helpful something that it was.
Wrongly trained it might have been as brilliant as the
lightning's flash, but also as destructive.

But this woman chose, all unwittingly, it is true,
to give her baby to be nursed by his own mother.
And this Jewish woman was not a heathen. She was
a faithful servant of the Lord. I can see her as she
hurries down to the banks of the Nile. And as she
goes there's a wonderful light in her eyes. And her
lips are moving, and she is saying, "Blessed be the
God of Abraham and of Isaac and of Israel, who has
heard the prayer of His servant and who has granted
the desire of her heart."

And I love to look again upon this scene. The
Egyptian princess is handing over the precious little
bundle of immortality into the arms of a Jewish slave.
And that Jewish slave is hugging her own child to her
hungry heart. And the princess is talking to her
proudly, haughtily, as becomes her rank, "Take this
child away and nurse him for me and I will give thee
thy wages." And away goes this mother, the happiest
mother, I think, in all the world.

Now, had you met this mother with her child
so wonderfully restored to her and had asked her
whose was the child and for whom she was nursing
it, I wonder what she would have said. I know what
the attendants of the princess thought. I know what
they would have said. They would have said that she

was nursing the child for the Princess. They would have said that the Princess was her employer. They would have said that Moses was the Princess's baby.

But this mother never thought of it in any such way. She laughed in the secret depths of her heart at the idea of her being employed by the Princess. Who was her employer? I know what she thought. She believed that God was. She had a pious fancy that God was speaking through the lips of that Princess and that He was saying, "Take the child and nurse him for me and I will give thee thy wages." She thought her child was God's child. Therefore, she believed that it was to God, and not to the Egyptian Princess, that she was to account at the last for the way in which she trained and played the mother's part by her boy.

Yes, I feel confident that this mother believed that God was her real employer. She believed that she was His minister. She believed that she had been chosen for the task that was now engaging her. And she was right in her belief. When God, who had great plans for Moses, sought for some one who was to make it possible for Him to realize His plans, whom did He choose? To whom did He commit this precious treasure, from whose life such infinite blessings should come to the world? He did not commit him to a heathen. He did not commit him to a mere hired servant. He committed him to his mother. When God wants to train a child for the achieving of the best and the highest in life He sends him to school to a godly mother.

Now, when God chose the mother of Moses for his nurse and his teacher He made a wise choice. The choice was wise, in the first place, because this mother of Moses was eager for her task. She was a willing mother. Whatever glad days may have come in her life history, I am sure no gladder time ever came than that time when she realized that to her was going to be given the matchless privilege of mothering her own child. I know there are some mothers who do not agree with her. I know there are some that look upon the responsibilities of motherhood as building a kind of prison, but not so this immortal mother. She looked upon her duty as her highest privilege. She entered upon her task with an eagerness born of a quenchless love.

The choice was fortunate, in the second place, because she was a woman of faith. In the letter to the Hebrews we read that Moses was hidden by faith. Both the father and the mother of Moses were pious people. They were people of consecration, of devotion to God, of faith in God. It is true they were slaves. It is true they had a poor chance. It is true they lived in a dark day when the light was dim, but they lived up to their light. And their home was a pious home and its breath was sweet and fragrant with the breath of prayer.

And I have little hope for the rearing of a great Christian leader in any other type of home. I have no hope of rearing a new and better civilization in any other type of home. Our national life is discordant and hate-torn to-day. We are living in a time of intense bitterness and selfishness and sordid greed. But what civilization is to-day, the home life of yesterday has made it. And what civilization will be to-morrow the home life of to-day will make it. If we do not have Christian homes, believe me, we will never have a Christian civilization.

"I know Abraham," God said, "that he will command his children and his household after him." And there are two remarkable assertions made of Abraham in this text. First, He said, "I know that Abraham will command; I know Abraham will control his own household. I know that Abraham will control his children." And God considered that as highly important. Of course we are too wise to agree with Him to-day. We believe it best to let our children run wild and do largely as they please. We believe that Solomon was an old fogey when he spoke of "sparing the rod and spoiling the child." And I am not here this morning to tell you just how you are to control your child. But what I do say is that you cannot commit a greater blunder than to fail to control it. A child is better unborn than untrained.

Then God said of Abraham next, not only that he would command his children and his household, but that he would command them after him. He would not only exercise the right kind of authority, but he would exert the right kind of influence. He would set the right kind of example. He knew that Abraham would be in some measure what he desired his children to be, that by authority and by right living he would Christianize his own home.

And so when God wanted to raise up a man Moses who was to remake the world, He put him in a pious home. He gave him a godly father and mother. And the dominant influence in the life of Moses was his mother. No woman ever did a greater work. But it was a work that she accomplished not because of her high social standing. Nor was it accomplished because of her great culture. It was accomplished because of her great faith.

And while I am not in any sense a pessimist, I cannot but tremble in some measure for the future because of the decay of home religion. And this decay, while traceable in some measure to the madness for money and pleasure among men, is traceable even more to this same madness among women. The woman of to-day is in a state of transition. She has not yet fully found herself. There has come to her a new sense of freedom, and this freedom has not made her better. She has become in considerable measure an imitator of man. And sad to say, she imitates his vices instead of his virtues. She often patterns after what is worst in him instead of what is best.

I am told that in the Woman's Club of this city the handsomest room in the building is the smoking room. Now, a woman has a right to smoke. Who says that she has not? A woman has a right to swear, and that right she is exercising with growing frequency. I am not going to deny her right to do that. But what I do say is this, that I have absolutely no hope for the rearing of a right generation at the hands of a flippant cigarette-smoking mother. The child of such a mother is, in my candid opinion, half damned in its birth. Remember, the mother of Moses was a pious mother. If she had not been I am persuaded that the Moses who has been one of the supreme makers of history, might never have been known.

Now, what was this woman's task? Hear it. I take these words as embodying not the will of the princess, but the will of God, "Take this child and nurse him for me and I will give thee thy wages." This mother was not to govern the world. She was not to lecture in the interest of suffrage. I have nothing to say against the woman who does so. She was not to be the center of a social set. She was not to turn her child over to some colored woman while she went gadding about to every sort of club. She had just one supreme job. She had one highest and holiest of all tasks. It was for that cause that she came into the world. She was to train her child for God. And whoever we are and whatever may be our abilities, we can have no higher task than this. The training of a child to-day is the biggest big job under the stars. He is the center of all our hopes and possibilities.

Did you ever read the story of the "Little Palace Beautiful"? In the Little Palace Beautiful there are four rooms. The first is a room called Fancy. In this room looking out toward the south sleeps a little child, a beautiful baby. It is the Child-that-Never-Was. It was longed for, hoped for, dreamed of, but it never came. In the west room looking out toward the sunset, the room called Memory, is the Child-that-Was. Here sleeps the little fellow that came and stayed just long enough to gather up all our heart's love and then he went away. In the room toward the north, the room of Experience, is the Child-that-Is. He is the little fellow that now plays in your home in your Sunday School class. And in the room looking out toward the sunrise, the room called Hope, is the Child-that-Is-to-Be.

Now, we are interested in all four of these children, but our interest in the four is to be expressed in our care for just one, and that is the Child-that-Is. We think tenderly of the Child-that-Never-Was. We think sadly of the Child-that-Was. But we bring the love that we might have given and did give, to lavish it upon the Child-that-Is. We think hopefully of the Child-that-Is-to-Be, but we realize that all his possibilities are locked in the Child-that-Is. And so the world's future salvation is in our cradles, in our homes and in our nurseries to-day. To train our Children for God is the highest of all high tasks.

And notice that this woman was to receive wages for her work. What were her wages? I suppose the princess sent down a little coin at the end of each week, but do you think that is all the pay that this mother got? I feel confident that she never counted this as pay at all. But she received her reward, she received her wages. And they were wages that were rich in worth beyond all our fondest dreams. First, there was given unto her the fine privilege of loving. And Paul, who knew what was priceless, Paul, who knew what was of supreme value, said that love was the soul's finest treasure. And he meant not the privilege of being loved, as fine as that is, but the higher privilege of loving. And it has been given by the grace of God to the mothers of men to be the world's greatest lovers.

> "If I were hanged on the highest hill,
>   Mother o' mine, O mother o' mine!
>   I know whose love would follow me still,
>   Mother o' mine, O mother o' mine!
>
> "If I were drowned in the deepest sea,
>   Mother o' mine, O mother o' mine!
>   I know whose tears would come down to me,
>   Mother o' mine, O mother o' mine!
>
> "If I were damned of body and soul,
>   I know whose prayers would make me whole,
>   Mother o' mine, O mother o' mine!"

To her was given, in the second place, the fine reward of self-sacrifice. She had the privilege of giving.

She had the privilege of offering her life a willing sacrifice upon the altar of her home. It is blessed to receive, but it is more blessed to give. And the rewards of motherhood are the highest rewards because she is the most godlike giver that this world knows.

Then, she was rewarded, in the third place, by the making of a great life. She became the mother of a good man. Her faith became his faith. "By faith Moses was hidden." That was by his mother's faith. But in the next verse we read this, "By faith Moses, when he was come to years, refused to be called the son of Pharaoh's daughter." That was by his own faith. Where did he get that rare jewel? He got it from the training of his mother. He saw it in her life. It looked out from her eyes. It spoke through her lips. He drank it in as he lay in her arms.

"When I call to remembrance the unfeigned faith that is in thee, which dwelt first in thy grandmother Lois and in thy mother Eunice, and I am persuaded is in thee also." Oh, if you are here a man of faith, a woman of faith, the chances are you secured that precious treasure at the hands of a God-loving and a God-trusting mother.

So this despised slave woman, this mother has this to her credit, that she mothered and trained one of the greatest men that ever set foot on this earth. She took a little boy named Moses to her heart and trained him for God. She had him for a little while. Then he went away to the big University. But he stood true. She speaks to him as she holds him close in the twilight. She says, "Laddie, do not forget how God has watched over you. One day when death was suspended above your baby head by a thread, one day when your life was frailer than a gossamer thread, I took a queer little basket and lined it with pitch, and also with faith and with prayer. And I put you afloat, and God preserved you and sent you back into these arms. And I carried you and cared for you. And now when you are grown you won't forget. You won't prove disloyal to your mother and you won't forget your mother's God."

And Moses did not forget. And one day the little laddie who had once been carried about in the arms of a slave mother, was a big broad-shouldered man. And he had a big broad-shouldered faith, and he trusted in a big broad-shouldered God. And in the strength of that faith, and in the might of that God he lifted an enslaved people in his arms and carried them clean across the wilderness. And he made possible an Isaiah and a Jeremiah and a David. And he made possible the birth of Jesus Christ. And he became the blesser and enricher of all the nations of the earth. And this mother, whose name is not well known in the annals of men, but whose name is known in Heaven to-day, had the rich reward of knowing that she mothered a man who fathered a nation and blessed a world.

Oh, it is a blessed reward, the reward of success in the high enterprise of motherhood. I know of no joy that can come to a father's or a mother's heart that is comparable to the joy that their own children can give them. I have seen sweet-faced mothers look upon their children when there was enough joy in those faces to have raised the temperature of Heaven.

But while it is true that none can bring us so much joy, it is also true that none can so utterly break our hearts. To see disease take our children in hand and wreck their bodies is painful, but it is as joy in comparison to seeing sin steal the moral rose from their

cheek and the sparkle of innocence and purity from
their eyes. But the deepest of all damning griefs is
that grief that comes to us when we realize that we
failed, and that their ruin is due to sin and unfaith-
fulness in ourselves.

Do you hear the wild outcry from that broken-hearted
king named David? There he stands upon the wall
and looks away across the wistful plain. A lone runner
is coming. He knows he is a messenger from the
battlefield. "Good tidings," he shouts. But the king
has no ear for good tidings. His one question is this,
"Is the young man Absalom safe?" And the runner
does not rightly answer his question. Then the second
messenger comes with the news of his son's death.
And there is no more pathetic cry in literature than
that that breaks from the lips of this pathetic king.
"O my son Absalom, O Absalom, my son, my son!"
He is sobbing over his lost boy. But there is an added
pang to his grief. It is the awful pang that comes
from the torturing fear that he himself is in large
measure responsible for the loss of his boy. And there
is no more bitter agony than that.

Oh, men and women, let us who are fathers and
mothers spare ourselves David's terrible agony. Let
us spare our children Absalom's tragic ruin. Let us give
ourselves the joys of this old time mother. While our
children are about us, may we hear the very voice of
God speaking to us on their behalf, saying: "Take this
child and train it for me and I will give thee thy
wages." And wages we shall receive just as surely as
did this mother of Moses. We will be privileged to
love, to give, to bless. And God Himself can give
no richer reward than that.

XV

A GOOD MAN'S HELL—MANASSEH

Jeremiah 15:4

"And I will cause them to be removed into all the kingdoms of the earth because of Manasseh." The prophet of the Lord is here fixing the responsibility for the downfall of Jerusalem. He says that the wreck was due in an especial sense to one man. He makes it very plain that it was one man's hands that had planted the infernal bomb that was destined in later years to blast the foundation from under the nation. "I will cause them to be removed into all the kingdoms of the earth because of Manasseh."

Had a jury at that day been impanelled to try this man Manasseh I do not know whether they would have found him guilty or not. Possibly they would. It is also possible that they would not. Had they failed to have done so it would have been because they did not know the facts; they were not entirely familiar with all the evidence in the case. But when God sought the man upon whose shoulders rested the chief responsibility for the wreck of the nation, He fixed on this man. When Manasseh stood on trial before Him, charged with the terrible crime of blasting a kingdom, he was found guilty.

It was a startling verdict. It is all the more startling when we realize that Manasseh in the last years of his life was a good man. It was only his earlier years that were spent in sin. In his old age he was a saint.

171

In the last years of his reign he knew God and did all that he could to undo the evils of an ill-spent yesterday. But in spite of the saintliness of the eventide, in spite of his winter-time goodness, the full influence of his life was not a blessing but a curse. It did not make for upbuilding. It made for terrible downfall and ruin.

Take a glance at his life's story. It is full of interest. Every young heart in the world should make a study of the life of this man. How it gives the lie to many of our false and easy conceptions of sin. How urgent it presses home the truth that the only salvation that can mean the most is the salvation that grips us from life's earliest moment to its very last.

Manasseh came to the throne when he was only twelve years of age. He had not been long in his position of influence and power till he turned utterly away from the Lord and began to wallow in every form of sin. There was no dirty idolatry that he did not practise. There was no false belief to which he did not seem willing to give hospitality. There was scarcely any form of evil of which he was not guilty.

And his career of godlessness was all the more inexcusable because of the good opportunities that he had. He was the son of a great and good father. His father was Hezekiah. And Hezekiah was one of the best kings that Judah ever had. He was a man of spiritual power. He was a man who served as saving salt to his kingdom throughout his entire reign. When the Assyrians hung like a threatening storm cloud over his weak little nation, it was the compelling might of his prayer that stood as a wall between them and their enemy. So, Manasseh was the son of a great saint.

And mark me, it is no small privilege to be the child of a godly father or of a saintly mother. If God granted to you to open your baby eyes to look into other eyes that were "homes of silent prayer," if He sent you to grow up in a home where the family altar and the saintly life made Christ real, then He has given you an opportunity unspeakably great. And as great as is your opportunity, just so great is your responsibility. How hard must be the sentence upon that boy or that girl who breaks away from such saving and sanctifying influences to go into the far country.

Not only was the guilt of Manasseh intensified by the fact that he had a saintly father. It was intensified further by the fact that he was repeatedly warned. Though he turned his back on God and though he gave himself up to a perfect orgy of wrong doing, God did not forget him and did not give him up. He sent to him messenger after messenger to bring home his guilt and to invite him back to the pardon and peace of his Father's presence. But seemingly the more he was warned the deeper he plunged into sin.

And you who are in sin, you are even more guilty than he, because to you God has sent warning after warning, rebuke after rebuke. God has given you calls and invitations without number. He has called you through your conscience. He has called you through your wretchedness and restlessness and hunger of heart. He has called you through your longing for usefulness. He has called you through your sorrow and your pain and your losses. He has called you through ten thousand mercies. Oh, believe me, our need to-night is not so much for more light as it is for courage to live up to the light we have.

Not only was Manasseh guilty because he sinned in

spite of the help of a godly father and in spite of repeated warnings. His guilt was deepened yet more because he knew that he did not sin alone. When he went away from God he carried a kingdom with him. The reign of Hezekiah had been a righteous reign. With the coming of Manasseh to the throne there was a violent reaction, akin to that that followed upon the restoration of Charles II to the throne of England. You know how that when Charles came to the throne the court life was changed into a brothel. Charles lived in open and notorious adultery, and the rotten-ness of the throne led to the rottenness of the kingdom. Such was the case here. Manasseh not only fell but he drew a kingdom after him.

It is profoundly true that no man ever sins alone. Your influence will not be so wide as that of Manasseh, yet however obscure your life may be this is true, that it will set in motion influences that will literally outlast the world. I have control over my own action before it is done, but after it is done I seek to control it in vain. If it is a fiendish act it laughs its devilish and derisive laughter in my face and says, "Control me if you can."

Now, there came a time when this great sinner began to pay the penalty for his sin. Retribution slipped in by the guards at the door one day and took the king rudely by the shoulder. It shook him and shook him so roughly that his crown fell from his head and his sceptre dropped from his hand. Then it dragged him from his throne and dressed him in chains and sent him a captive into a foreign country.

Retribution, suffering for sin, does not always come as it came to this king. It does not always come at once but come it does. That is as sure as the fact of

God. There are some shallow souls that fancy that because sin does not pay off every Saturday night that it does not pay at all. But to hold such views is to spit in the face of a most open and palpable fact. Manasseh had a fancy that he was a much freer man than his father had been, far more broad-minded, but he waked one day, as every man wakes sooner or later, to discover that sin did not mean freedom, that it only meant slavery.

Now, what effect did this degradation and shame and suffering have on the king? Suffering has very opposite influences on different types of character. Sometimes it hardens us, it makes us only the more bitter and rebellious. But suffering did not have that effect on Manasseh. It made him think, and it is a tremendously good day when God can get a man to think. He thought, I dare say, of his saintly father. He thought of his father's God. This story is another evidence of how all but impossible it is for a child to break finally away from the saving influence of a truly good father or truly good mother.

This experience not only made him think but it sent him to his knees in an agony of prayer. He came to hate the sin that had been the ruin of him. He asked God for forgiveness. And God did forgive him. Truly, "though your sins be as scarlet, they shall be as white as snow." No man ever goes so far away from God, no man ever lives in sin so long but that if he will return to God, God will receive him and will give him abundant pardon.

Not only did God save this man. He brought him again to his throne. And he who had once been a captive in a strange land wore his crown once more. And for the remaining years of his life he was a devout follower of the Lord. He did his best to undo the evils of the earlier years of his reign. He tore down the altars to false gods that he had builded. He tried to bring his people back to the new and saving faith that he had found. His conversion was genuine and lasting.

But what was the result? He did not succeed. He found that it was easier to lead folks astray than it was to bring them back after he had led them astray. He was a good man. He knew God. But this was his hell, that he had to stand in utter helplessness and see his nation totter to its ruin because of the sins that he had committed. He was not even able to save his own home. His boy became a godless idolater, as he himself had been during the best years of his life.

So we are brought face to face with this fact. Repentance will bring us salvation whenever we repent, but there is one thing that repentance cannot do. It cannot save us from the consequences of our sin. Go out into the field of life and sow tares for half a century, if you dare. Even then God will forgive you if you will come in repentance to Him, but there is one thing that God will not do and cannot do. He cannot change the tares that you have sown into wheat. I may be exceedingly sorry for my wrong sowing, I will be, but the seed will grow none the less.

Did it ever occur to you how many faces the Prodigal missed on his way back home? Many a splendid young fellow that caroused with him as he went into the far country did not enjoy the fatted calf with him when he came back to the peace and plenty of his Father's house. Some of them had gone into eternity and others had gone beyond his influence forever more.

While I was in Huntington a few weeks ago, the

pastor for whom I was preaching told me of a young friend of his who carried his little baby in to see a noted eye specialist. The child's eyes were very bad. The physician examined them and shook his head. "Her eyes will never get better," he said, "but will get worse. She will be blind before she is grown." And the father's face went white and he said, "Doctor, you know my youth wasn't what it ought to have been. Can that be the cause?" And the doctor said, "You needn't to have told me. Certainly it is the cause." And it was a broken-hearted man that left that office that day. And it was a broken-hearted and praying and penitent man that kissed his child to sleep that night. Oh, God will forgive him, but there is one thing that that forgiveness will not include and that is daylight for his little girl.

"I will cause them to be removed into all the kingdoms of the earth because of Manasseh." And Manasseh is good and pure and blood-washed, but the influences that he set in motion have gone beyond his reach forever more. What a fearful fact is this! I am talking to young men and women and you have your lives before you. You may give them to sin, and you may be saved at the last moment. That is a possibility, though it is a slight one. But such a salvation may mean the wrecking of many another life. The only safe way is to repent before you waste your life. Repent before you sin.

Do you remember Esau's pathetic story? He sold his birthright for one mess of lentils. Nor was he at all displeased with his bargain. At least that was true for a little while, but there came a time when he was sorry. There came a time when his foolish bartering broke his heart. And the story says that he found no place for repentance though he sought it diligently and with tears.

That does not mean, of course, that God refused to forgive Esau. The moment we turn in penitent surrender to our Lord He will save us and give us an abundant pardon, however far we may have gone into sin. God forgave him when he repented, but there was one thing that his repentance could not do. It could not undo the past. It could not put him again in the light of the morning of life. It could not place in his hands the opportunities of yesterday. The good that he might have done and the service that he might have rendered and the crowns that he might have won had passed beyond the reach of his hand forever. Repentance saved his soul but it did not save his life.

And what a startling chapter is the story of the sin of David. David was a whole-hearted man. He never did anything by halves. When he sinned he sinned with a horrible abandon. Few men have dirtier pages in their life's history than that of David's sin against the house of Uriah. But as his sin was whole-hearted so also was his repentance. We can hear his heart-broken cry for pardon across the centuries: "Have mercy upon me, O God, according to thy loving kindness. According unto the multitude of thy tender mercies blot out my transgressions. Wash me from my iniquity and cleanse me from my sin; for I acknowledge my transgression and my sin is ever before me." It is the heart-broken cry of the penitent who has not one good word to say for himself. And God heard his prayer and washed him and made him whiter than snow.

But beyond that God with all His love and tenderness could not go. He could not save David from the consequences of his sin. His bloody and lustful deed became possessed of a power beyond his control. "Down!" he cries to it in helpless horror. But it will not down. "Then where are you going?" he asks, all a-tremble with dread. And the fiendish deed answers, "I am going to steal the purity of your daughter Tamar. I am going to make your son Ammon into a rapist. I am going to make your handsome boy Absalom into a murderer."

When I was a boy there was a family living neighbors to us, all of whom were outside the Church. But when the children were almost all grown and the father was an old man he became a Christian. But instead of being influential in bringing his children to Christ they seemed only to be ashamed of him. He did not seem to have the slightest power to influence a single one of them for good. I would not say that he was not saved, I think he was, but I think his years spent in sin cost him the salvation of his children.

E. J. Bulgin said that he was holding a meeting some years ago in a city in Kentucky. A girl was converted in his meeting. She was in the early bloom of young womanhood. She belonged to a wealthy and prominent family. Her mother was not a Christian. The girl wanted to join the Church and the mother objected. The preacher went to see the mother and prayed with her and plead with her. She said she wanted her daughter to have her coming out dance soon and therefore she should not join the Church. And the preacher left that home with a heavy heart.

Three years later he was holding a meeting in a neighboring town. A long distance call came asking him if he would not come and conduct the funeral of Nellie, the girl who had not been allowed to join the

Church. He went. The undertaker said that it was a request of the mother that the preacher ride with her and her other daughter to the cemetery. The journey was made in silence. The remains were being lowered when the mother ordered the undertaker to open the coffin again. All the crowd was requested to stand back. They moved some fifty feet away. Then leaning on the preacher's arm the mother showed him her daughter. And lying upon her breast was a little armful of shame.

That was all. The grave was filled and on the way back home the penitent and heart-broken mother found Christ. She said to her daughter, "Mary, I have found Jesus. I have found the salvation that I rejected three years ago." And Mary answered, "No, Mother, you have found salvation, it is true. But it is not the salvation that was offered to you three years ago. Your salvation then would have included the salvation of Nellie. Now it means only the salvation of yourself."

Heart, you may be saved at another time. Many a father is saved after he has wrecked his boys. This mother was saved after she had destroyed her daughter. Manasseh was saved after he had ruined his kingdom. But I submit to you that it is not the largest salvation. It is a salvation that may yet leave you with a burning hell in your own heart, the hell of the memory of evil you can never undo, and wrongs you can never right, and of lost men and women, led away from God by your influence that you can never lead back again.

Therefore, because of these startling and palpable facts, I come to you with this oft-repeated word of our Lord upon my lips: "Now is the accepted time. To-day is the day of salvation." Seek not to make

religion into a fire escape.   Give God your life now
and in so doing you will both save yourself and those
who are influenced by you.   "Therefore, choose you this
day whom you will serve."

XVI

A SHREWD FOOL—THE RICH FARMER

Luke 12:16-21

"And he spake a parable unto them, saying, The ground of a certain rich man brought forth plentifully: and he thought within himself, saying, What shall I do, because I have no room where to bestow my fruits? And he said, This will I do: I will pull down my barns and build greater and there will I bestow all my fruits and my goods. And I will say to my soul, Soul, thou hast much goods laid up for many years; take thine ease, eat, drink, and be merry. But God said unto him, Thou fool, this night thy soul shall be required of thee: then whose shall those things be, which thou hast provided? So is he that layeth up treasure for himself, and is not rich toward God."

I count with confidence on your interest in this sermon. You will be interested, in the first place, because the picture that our Lord has given us in this wonderful story is the picture of a real man. This farmer is no wax figure. He is no bloodless nonentity. He is altogether human stuff. And we are interested in real folks.

Then we are interested in this man, in the second place, because he is successful. We are naturally interested in the people who make good. If you go out on the street to-morrow and start to tell your friends how you failed, the chances are that they will turn their backs upon you to listen to the man, with triumph in his face and victory in his voice, who is telling how he succeeded. We are great success worshippers. And the man who wins the prizes of life interests us very keenly.

But there is a shock for us in the story. The Master calls our shrewd hero a fool. "Thou fool." That is a harsh and jarring word. It insults us. It shakes its fist in our faces. It cuts us like a whip. It offends us. We do not like the ugly name in the least.

"Thou fool." Our Master frowns upon our using such language at all. He will not trust us with such a sharp sword. He will not suffer us to hurl such a thunderbolt. He forbids us, under a terrible penalty, to call our brother a fool. And yet He calls this keen and successful farmer a fool. And He doesn't do so lightly and flippantly, but there seems to ring through it scorn and indignation—positive anger, anger that is all the more terrible because it is the anger of love.

Why did the Master call this man a fool? He did not get the idea from the man himself. This well-to-do farmer would never have spoken of himself in that way. He regarded himself as altogether fit and mentally well furnished. Nor did the Master get His idea from the man's neighbors. They looked upon this man with admiration. There may have been a bit of envy mingled with their admiration, but they certainly did not regard him as a fool. They no more did so than we regard the man that is like him as a fool to-day.

Why then did the Master label him with this ugly name? It was not because he had a prejudice against him. Jesus was no soured misanthrope. He was no snarling cynic. He did not resent a man just because he had made a success. He was not an I. W. W. growling over real or fancied wrongs. No, the reason that Jesus called him a fool is because no other name would exactly fit him.

It is well, however, that the Master labeled this picture. Had He not done so you and I might have been tempted to put the wrong label on it. We might have labeled it "The Wise Man," or some such fine name. But had we done so it would have been a colossal blunder. Had we done so I am persuaded that the very fiends would have howled with derisive laughter. For when we see this man as he really is, when we see him through the eyes of Him who sees things clearly, then we realize that there is only one name that will exactly fit him. Then we know that that one name is the short ugly one by which he is called—"Fool."

But why is he a fool? In what does his foolishness consist? Certainly it does not consist in the fact that he has made a success. He is not a fool simply because he is rich. The Bible is a tremendously reasonable book. It is the very climax of sanity. It is the acme of good common sense. It never rails against rich men simply because they are rich. It no more does that than it lauds poor men because they are poor. It frankly recognizes the danger incident to the possession of riches. It makes plain the fact that the rich man is a greatly tempted man. But never is he condemned simply because he is rich.

The truth of the matter is that riches in themselves are counted neither good nor bad, neither moral nor immoral. The Bible recognizes money as a real force. What is done with this force depends upon the one who controls it. Money is condensed energy. It is pent-up power. It is lassoed lightning. It is a Niagara that I can hold in my hand and put into my pocket. It is a present day Aladdin's lamp. If I possess this lamp a million genii stand ready to do my bidding. Whatever service I demand, that will they do, whether that service look toward the making of men or the wrecking of men.

In case I live for self they are able to assist me in all my selfish enterprises. They can provide a winter palace in the city and a summer palace in the mountains or down by the sea. They can adorn my walls with the choicest of paintings. They can put the finest of carpets upon my floors. They can make possible tours abroad and private boxes at the theatre. They can search the treasure houses of the world and bring to me their rarest jewels. They can give me a place among the select four hundred, with whole columns about myself in the society page of the Metropolitan Daily.

Even this is not all. If I, their master, am so minded, these powerful genii will defeat for me the ends of justice. They will override the constitution. They will enable me to put a stain upon the very flag of my own country. They will make it possible for me at times to disregard the rights of others. When occasion demands they may even purchase at my desire the honor of manhood and the virtue of womanhood.

On the other hand, if I am a good man, I may set these genii to the doing of tasks great and worthwhile. I may command them to give clothing to the naked and food to the hungry. I can order them to build better schools for the education of the world. I can compel them to build better churches for the worship of God. I can send them with a chance in their hands for the unfortunate and the handicapped. I can make it impossible for one to say of that bright lad:—

> "But knowledge to his eyes her ample scroll,
> Rich with the spoils of time, did ne'er unroll.
> Chill penury suppressed his noble rage,
> And froze the genial current of the soul."

In fact there is no high task that man is called upon to perform but that these mighty genii can be of assistance. They can help "to heal the broken-hearted, to preach deliverance to the captives, and recovering of sight to the blind, to set at liberty them that are bruised." They can even make their master friends who will one day receive him into everlasting habitations.

> "Dug from the mountain side, washed in the glen,
> Servant am I of the Master of men.
> Earn me, I bless you; steal me, I curse you;
> Grip me and hold me, a fiend shall possess you.
> Lie for me, die for me, covet me, take me,
> Angel or devil, I am what you make me."

Nor was this man a fool because he had accumulated his money dishonestly. The man who does accumulate money dishonestly is a fool. So says the prophet Jeremiah and every clear thinking man must agree with him. There is a way of getting money that makes money a curse rather than a blessing. There is a way of getting money that makes the very eagle upon it to turn vulture to tear at your heart.

But this man had not made his money after that fashion. He had never run a saloon nor a gambling house nor a sweatshop. There is no hint that he had failed to pay an adequate wage to his laborers. James calls upon the rich men of his day to weep and howl because they were guilty in this respect. But no such charge as this is laid against this man. Nor had he robbed the widow or the fatherless. "An orphan's curse will drag to hell a spirit from on high," but no such curse was on this man.

How had he made his money? He had made it in a way that is considered the most honest and upright that is possible. He had made his money farming. Listen: "The ground of a certain rich man brought forth plentifully." The ground. It smacks of cleanliness, honesty, uprightness.

"The ground of a certain rich man brought forth plentifully." And when I read that I am back on the old farm again. As I read it there comes before me a vision of my boyhood's home. I see the old white house under the hill. I see the sturdy apple trees in front of it and the forest of beech, oak and chestnut stretching away in the distance back of it. I can hear the lowing of the cattle and the neighing of the horses and the crowing of the cock in the barnyard. I can hear the call of the bob white to his mate, and the song of the catbird in the thicket at the end of the row. I can feel the caress of the fresh upturned sod upon my bare feet. I can catch the fragrance of the new mown hay. I can see myself coming home in the gloaming "as the day fades into golden and then into gray and then into deep blue of the night sky with its myriad of stars that blossom at twilight's early hour like lilies on the tomb of day." And when I come home I come to a night of restful sleep because I have come from a clean day's work. No, this man was not a fool because he had gotten his money dishonestly. He had made it honestly, every dollar of it.

Nor was he a fool because he set about thoughtfully to save what he had made. The Bible sets no premium upon wastefulness. God lets us know that to waste anything of value is not only foolish but wicked. What was the sin of the Prodigal Son? It was this, that he "wasted his substance with riotous living." He spent his treasure without getting any adequate return.

That is the tragedy of a great number of us. I do not charge you with outrageous and disgraceful wickedness. But it is true that you are not investing your life in the highest possible way. You are squandering yourself on things of secondary value. And to you God is speaking as he spoke centuries ago: "Wherefore do you spend your money for that which is not meat and your labor for that which satisfieth not?" You have no right to waste yourself and you have just as little right to waste your money which represents a part of yourself.

No, the foolishness of this man was not in the fact that he sought to save what he had made. That is right. That is sensible. To do otherwise is at once wicked and little. Big things do not waste. This is a big world on which we live but it has never lost one single drop of water nor one single grain of sand since God flung it into space. And even Jesus Christ himself, the Lord of the universe, commanded His disciples after He had fed the multitude, to gather up the fragments that nothing be lost.

Why then, I repeat, does Christ call this man a fool? His foolishness lay fundamentally in the fact that he was a practical atheist. He had absolutely no sense of God. He lived as if the fact of God were an absolute lie. I do not think for a moment that he claimed to be an atheist. I have no doubt that he was altogether orthodox. I have no doubt that he went to the synagogue or to the temple every Sabbath day. But practically he was an utter atheist. And what is true of him is equally true of many another man who stands up every Sunday in Church to recite his creed.

How do we know that he is an atheist? We know it by hearing him think. Listen: "He thought within himself." Now then we are going to get to see this man as he really is. You can't always tell what a man is by the way he looks. He may look like the flower, but be the serpent under it. He may smile and smile, as Hamlet tells us, and be a villain. You can't always tell what he is by what he says. He may speak high sentiments to which his heart is a stranger. Nor can you tell him by what he does. He may "do his alms" simply to be seen of men. But if you can get in behind the scenes and see him think, then you will know him. Tell me, man, what you think within yourself and I will tell you what you are. For, "As a man thinketh in his heart, so is he."

Now, what did this man think? "He thought within himself, saying, What shall *I* do for *I* have no room where to bestow *My* goods and *My* fruits? And he said, This will *I* do. *I* will pull down *My* barns and build greater, and there will *I* bestow all *My* goods and *My* fruits." Now we see him. When he thought, he had not one single thought of God. God was as completely ignored as if He had no existence at all. This was the very fountain source of his foolishness. He reckoned without God, and the man who reckons without God is a fool.

Look now how this fatal foolishness casts its blight over his entire character. Reckoning without God, of course, he has no sense of Divine ownership. Quite naturally, therefore, he thinks because he possesses a farm, he owns a farm. Possession and ownership mean exactly the same thing to a man who begins by ignoring God. When you hear this man talk you find that the only pronouns he has in his vocabulary are "I," "My" and "Mine." He knows only the grammar of atheism. He is acquainted only with the vocabulary of the fool. "His" and "Ours" and "Yours" are not found in the fool's vocabulary.

Faith, on the other hand, makes large use of the word "His." It recognizes the fact that "the earth is the Lord's and the fullness thereof." It believes in the big truth: "Ye are not your own. You are bought with a price." Faith, taking God into consideration, wisely reckons that you are His and that all that you possess is His. It does not concede to you the ownership of anything. And for any man anywhere to-day to claim that because he possesses a farm or a bank or a brain, that, therefore, he owns it is to talk not the language of a wise man but the language of a fool.

This farmer's reckoning without God not only led him to confuse possession and ownership. It also robbed him of his gratitude. Crops were abundant. The farmer has prospered wonderfully. But leaving God out of his thinking there is no one for this farmer to thank for his success but himself. He never thought of taking hold of his sluggish soul and shaking it into wakefulness with this wise word, "Bless the Lord, O my soul, and forget not all His benefits." He did not concede the Lord any part in it.

There are many men just like him to-day. I was pastor in a small town some years ago. There was in that town only one rich man. He had made the money that he possessed, and they called him a self-made man. One day a certain preacher, not myself, went to him to ask him for a donation for some charity. He began by reminding this man of wealth how the Lord had blessed him. And what was the reply? It was about the meanest I ever heard. He said, "I know the Lord has blessed me, but I was there."

"I was there." And what he meant by that was that in reality the Lord had had nothing to do with it. "I did it all myself. In fact, if the Lord hadn't made the world I would. So there is not a thing for which I ought to be thankful." Now, the man who has no gratitude is a fool. He is a fool because the right sort of thinking always leads to thanking. The only kind of thinking that does not do so is the thinking of the practical atheist, and the practical atheist is a fool.

Then this farmer had no sense of obligation. This, too, is a natural outcome of his reckoning without God. Here is a man who is looking out on this same world upon which the farmer is looking, and he says, "I am a debtor both to the Greek and to the barbarian, both to the wise and to the unwise." The reason Paul says that is because he believes in God. God has blessed him and saved him with a wonderful salvation. Because of that fact he feels himself under infinite obligation to preach the Gospel that has saved himself. But this man, this fool, has only himself to thank for his prosperity. Therefore he has a right to use his wealth as he pleases. The man who has no sense of obligation, the man who tells you that he has a right to do as he pleases with his possessions is proclaiming to you not a new rule of ethics. He is simply telling you in unmistakable language that he is a fool.

This man showed himself a fool, last of all, by the confidence that he placed in things. Ignoring God he sought to find a substitute for God in abundant crops. He undertook to treat his soul as he would treat his sheep and his goats. Here he was, an immortal man. Here he was, destined to live when this old world has been a wreck for billions of years. And what provision does he make for himself? The same that he makes for his horses and his oxen and his asses. Of course, as one has pointed out, it was not foolish for him to make some provision for the few years he might live here. He was a fool for refusing to make provision for the eternity that he must live.

"Soul, thou hast much goods laid up for many days. Eat, drink and be merry." Did ever you hear words that were more stamped with moral idiocy? You can see from them that his soul has not fared well up to this time. You can easily tell from these words that his moral nature has been starved and stunted. We can easily tell that all his gettings have not satisfied him in the past. And yet he is vainly expecting satisfaction in the future. Now it is obvious that the man who forgets God, who turns aside to the worship of things, plays the fool.

So you see why the Master calls this shrewd farmer a fool. He began by reckoning without God. He virtually said in his heart, "There is no God." He went wrong in the very center of his nature. This put the blight of moral imbecility on his whole life. He turned to his possessions and sought to satisfy his soul with them. He received them without gratitude and held them without any sense of obligation, for he thought to possess was to own.

Now the Master, lest we should pull our skirts about us and thank God that we are not as this man, forces the truth home upon our own hearts. "So," He says, "is he that layeth up treasure for himself and is not rich toward God." That is, just the same kind of fool and just as big a fool is that man to-day who reckons without God and lives only for himself. If you are living your life in selfishness, however respectable that selfishness may be, you are just the same kind of fool and just as great a fool as is this rich man of the story.

Now the tragedy of this story, I take it, is that the foolishness of this farmer was self-chosen. His riches might have been a blessing to him here and a blessing through all eternity. In spite of the fact that he was rich in this world's goods he might also have been, in the truest sense, rich toward God. In fact, he might have been richer toward God with his wealth than without it. With it he might have exercised a far larger usefulness than he could have done without it. But he chose to ignore God and to rob himself and thus brand himself a fool now and evermore.

Don't forget that you and I may make the same tragic wreck of our lives. The only way to avoid doing so is to go right where this man went wrong. There is a sure road to spiritual enrichment. "Though he were rich, yet for our sakes he became poor that we, through his poverty, might be rich." This wealth is no fabled bag of gold at the end of the rainbow. I can so direct you to this treasure that you will be sure to find it. This is the road: "Yield yourselves unto God." That is your first duty. That is your highest wisdom. Recognize God as owner of yourself. Recognize God as the owner of all that you have. Give all to Him and He will give all to you. "For He that spared not His own Son, but delivered him up for us all, how shall He not with him also freely give us all things." To have that treasure is to be rich forever more. To be thus rich is to be eternally wise.